## PRAISE FOR *LETTERS TO A YOUNG ATHLETE*

"On the court, Chris Bosh was a rare superstar who put his team above himself. His book is a wise, candid look behind the scenes at what made him great and how he made others even greater. It should be required reading for up-and-coming athletes—and their parents, teachers, and coaches too."
—Adam Grant, #1 *New York Times* bestselling author of *Think Again* and host of the TED podcast *WorkLife*

"Chris Bosh, one of the smartest pro athletes of my life . . . goes deep on so many topics. . . . [*Letters to a Young Athlete*] is so smart, so thoughtful."
—Colin Cowherd

"CB was the ultimate teammate and competitor. As his coach, I learned so much about leadership, sacrifice, and persevering through great challenges and adversity. His basketball experiences are deep and loaded with life lessons. Whether you want to improve as an athlete or just gain more thoughtful perspective on this game of life, you will be inspired by this book!"
—Coach Erik Spoelstra

"Chris Bosh understands the complex reality of becoming a champion, and his book will show you how to navigate those challenges and win."
—Tim S. Grover

"*Letters to a Young Athlete* is a thoughtful, helpful manual for aspiring athletes to follow. The strength of the individual is the team and the strength of the team is the individual. Chris Bosh says all that and more to young athletes."
—Phil Jackson

PENGUIN BOOKS

# LETTERS TO A YOUNG ATHLETE

Chris Bosh fell in love with basketball at an early age and earned the prestigious "Mr. Basketball" title while still at Lincoln High School in Dallas, Texas. A McDonald's All-American, Bosh was selected fourth overall by the Toronto Raptors after one year attending Georgia Tech. In March 2019, Bosh's #1 jersey was officially retired for the Miami Heat. In addition to his basketball career, in 2010 he founded Team Tomorrow as a community-uplift organization. Bosh regularly speaks to youths about the benefits of reading, coding, and leadership. Bosh, his wife, Adrienne, and their five children reside in Austin, Texas.

# LETTERS TO A
# YOUNG ATHLETE

## CHRIS BOSH

FOREWORD BY PAT RILEY

PENGUIN BOOKS

PENGUIN BOOKS
An imprint of Penguin Random House LLC
penguinrandomhouse.com

First published in the United States of America by Penguin Press,
an imprint of Penguin Random House LLC, 2021
Published in Penguin Books 2022

ISBN 9781984881809 (paperback)

THE LIBRARY OF CONGRESS HAS CATALOGED THE HARDCOVER EDITION AS FOLLOWS:
Names: Bosh, Chris, 1984– author.
Title: Letters to a young athlete / Chris Bosh.
Description: New York : Penguin Press, [2021] | Includes index. |
Identifiers: LCCN 2020036671 (print) | LCCN 2020036672 (ebook) |
 ISBN 9781984881786 (hardcover) | ISBN 9781984881793 (ebook) |
Subjects: LCSH: Bosh, Chris, 1984– | Basketball players—United
 States—Biography. | Basketball players—United States—Conduct of life. |
 Basketball—United States—Vocational guidance.
Classification: LCC GV884.B658 A3 2021 (print) | LCC GV884.B658 (ebook) |
 DDC 796.323092 [B]—dc23
LC record available at https://lccn.loc.gov/2020036671
LC ebook record available at https://lccn.loc.gov/2020036672

Printed in the United States of America
10  9  8  7  6  5  4

BOOK DESIGN BY LUCIA BERNARD

I'd like to dedicate this book to my wonderful wife, Adrienne, and our five amazing children. There's nothing without you all and I love you with all my heart. To everyone who has helped me through this great journey so far: every coach, teacher, teammate, tutor, and supporter. Thank you.

# CONTENTS

FOREWORD BY PAT RILEY  xi

Introduction  1

LETTER 1 | When You Ain't Nothing but Tired  11

LETTER 2 | You Have to Find Your Why (and It
Can't Be Fame or Money)  29

LETTER 3 | The Gift of Hunger  44

LETTER 4 | Cultivating the Mind  55

LETTER 5 | Communication Is Key  72

LETTER 6 | Sweep Away Your Ego  91

LETTER 7 | Leaders Lead  109

LETTER 8 | Take Care of Yourself  124

LETTER 9 | Don't Let 'Em Get to You  140

LETTER 10 | The Name on the Front of the
Jersey Is What Counts  158

LETTER 11 | Winning and Losing: Not Too High,
Not Too Low  174

LETTER 12 | Do the Work. Do. The. Work.  194

Conclusion  211

ACKNOWLEDGMENTS  221

INDEX  223

# FOREWORD

BY PAT RILEY

Dear Chris,

There are decisive moments in your life that change everything for you and the people around you, moments when deep truths become crystal clear. On any day of your life a moment like that can happen. We become connected forever to these moments; they open the way to more and even greater experiences.

As a player, coach, and executive in the NBA for many years, I have experienced so many joyous and painful moments. They are never far from me: Going about my life, there will always be something that happens—a meeting, a call with a friend, a song, a picture on a wall—and I'm right back there again, often seeing the moment with more clarity and insight.

Some moments still seem incredible to me; I still think, "How did that happen?" A prime example is what I think of as your defining moment as a member of the Miami Heat. A year after winning your first championship with the Heat in 2012, against a great OKC team anchored by Russell Westbrook, James Harden, and Kevin Durant, we found ourselves in a real battle with the San Antonio Spurs trying to defend our title. San Antonio was a great team, coached by the venerable Gregg Popovich and led by Tim Duncan, Tony Parker, and Manu Ginobili. The Spurs were up three games to two and were ready to close us out on our home court to win the title. They had outplayed us to this point. Now, it was late in Game 6, and things looked very bleak for us: We were down 95–92 with 17 seconds to go. We had the ball and were attacking their defense. They needed one stop on defense and one rebound, and the game would have, for all intents and purposes, been over. We needed a score—a three or a two, anything to just keep us alive. Coach Spo set up a high double screen for LeBron, who got a great look at a three to tie the game. The clock was winding down under 10 seconds. LeBron missed, and the ball caromed off the rim and bounced very high. This is a make-or-miss league, but there are no coincidences. Now both teams needed a rebound. If SA rebounded the ball, we would have to foul. As the ball was in the air, our fans, who were all standing, started to boo the arena staff, who were already beginning to put out yellow rope to cordon off the court in anticipation of an SA win.

The ball seemed to take forever to come down. The SA defense had switched every screen, and you ended up being played by Tony Parker, a bad rebounding matchup for SA, as you had ten inches in height over him. You were such a smart, intuitive player. You knew you had the advantage, you just needed to make sure you did not oversize the match-up opportunity and get called for an offensive foul on Parker's block out by pushing him. With exquisite timing, you jumped as high as you could after the ball. You did not wait for the ball to come to you. You had great hands, like a vise; you grabbed the ball with very little time on the clock, and with great poise found the most dangerous three-point shooter in the history of the NBA. Ray Allen had been here before. Anticipating that you would get that rebound, Ray began to blindly backpedal to the corner. After years of doing these kinds of things, his court awareness was spot-on. "Ball in the air, feet in the air" was a coaching phrase that I used a lot in teaching the fundamentals of meeting the pass for a shot so you would be on balance. Ray caught the ball as he planted his feet perfectly behind the three-point line. Right off his toes he leapt in the air, squared his body to the basket, eyes laser-like in their focus on the rim, and let it fly. His follow-through was complete as three Spurs players ran desperately toward him to get a decent contest on the shot. I was standing right behind Ray, thinking that we got a great look by LeBron, we got a saving offensive rebound by you, and we got a pinpoint assist by you, the perfect pass right into the soft hands of our best clutch shooter, Ray Allen. In this dire situation you could not ask for anything more. Make or miss! The crowd was in a petrified state, eyes closed, mouths opened in an Oh My God look, praying for a miracle moment. With 5.3 seconds left on the clock, the ball went in, tying the game 95–95 and inciting the pure, thunderous delirium of a home crowd going crazy. Oh my! The feeling of that adrenaline hit, and the momentum shift in the minds of the players is hard to describe. Our players were not going to let that moment slip by.

At the end of overtime, up by one, *we* needed a final stop. The Spurs set up a play for Danny Green, who was their Ray Allen. It was a multidirectional play with a lot of player movement and screens. As the ball was passed to the weak-side corner, Green was open to catch it, but you recognized the late switch and closed on him hard. When Green jumped to shoot, you—with great timing and without fouling—blocked the shot, sealing our win. Those dreadful gold ropes disappeared. There would be no SA celebration in Miami that night. Your rebound, assist to Ray, and blocked shot on Green showed everyone your versatility and greatness, the spirit and heart to do the little things that win games when it counts. Two nights later the Miami Heat went on to win Game 7 at home and celebrate another championship. LeBron was the Finals MVP, deservingly. All the players who played in that series had their moments, but for anyone who knows anything about winning, and coming up big, you will go down in Miami Heat history as the player who made the greatest sequence of plays ever to assure a championship. There are no coincidences. Chris Bosh forever.

## AGONY

Flash back to two years earlier. You looked up at the scoreboard, defeated and perplexed, then sighed deeply while taking in the sight of the Dallas Mavericks celebrating winning the 2011 NBA championship. And yes, on our home court, making this loss even more dreadful. With head down, shoulders slumped, you slowly meandered through the crowded floor and down Championship Alley at American Airlines Arena. I could see a man in great pain. Watching all of your championship dreams go up in a Dirk Nowitzki fusillade of soft jumpers and Jason Kidd smart plays was the worst professional experience of your life. You dropped to your knees and wept deeply. Your teammates put hands on your back and consoled you as best they could, then scooped you up and walked slowly to the locker room arm in arm, brothers feeling the same pain.

In winner-take-all scenarios like the NBA Finals, some players deal with loss stoically, some depressively, some angrily. Some seem to treat it matter-of-factly, as if it is just another loss, while others fall apart and let the tears flow. The incredible swing in emotions is hard to describe, especially if you really care. In any case, losing makes for a really bad summer. A lot of players just go down the rabbit hole and don't come out for weeks. These failures really never leave you until the ball starts to bounce again in the fall. Observing this sad moment, I was left feeling that I did not do enough to help you all win. It was the worst feeling I'd felt in a long time. But I have been through these shattering moments many times before. Please, pull the blanket of despair over my head and make this nightmare disappear. PLEASE! . . . But no blanket or hot shower will wash the pain away. Time will, and you come back. Pull yourself up by those old bootstraps because that's what pros do. And you were the consummate pro.

Just a year before, on July 9, 2010, a massive celebration took place in the same arena to introduce Miami to "the Big Three." LeBron James, our own Dwyane Wade, and you had decided to sign with the Miami Heat together as a "superteam." On stage, with so much joy and love streaming at him from thousands of Heat fans, LeBron effusively stated that this team could win not one, not two, not three, not four, but many championships. You could hardly blame him for being swept up in the moment, but some people did, and so when, one year later, with all the chips on the line, we were humiliated by Dallas at home, the pain was deep. LeBron took most of the heat from the critics because he did not play up to their or his expectations. People declared the Big Three finished before we even got started.

Dallas stuck it to us good. The media coverage was ugly. This is what most everyone wanted to see, a Big Three loss. A bad one. They got it. Now, how were we going to deal with it? What changes would have to be made going into the next year? The ramifications of that loss would direct us to change. As I have always said, there are two states of emotion in sports: There is winning and there is misery, and nothing in between. These wounds would heal, and you had a lot to do with applying the necessary salve.

You are smart as hell and a very sensible, pragmatic individual. More than that, you have a remarkable character that is an unusual combination of compassion and mental toughness. That combination helped us to build a truly great team.

It started with great individual sacrifice, on and off the court. You sacrificed the most on the court by relinquishing shots, points, touches—*your* game—to Dwyane and LeBron. Dwyane sacrificed his own game to enhance the opportunities for the team's best player, LeBron. LeBron flourished in this number-one role, and the team's new pecking order jelled, without any of the ego problems that often occur from these sorts of asks. You, LeBron, and Dwyane consciously and unselfishly embraced the attitude of real winners together, sharpening the focus away from the "whose team it is" department and eliminating the individual competitive edges and egos that bring great teams down. It was a whole new ball game: We not only had superstars but also very intelligent players who were motivated to win championships, not scoring titles. The sportsmanship was there from the beginning: We had players who were great at their sport and classy as individuals. But deep inside your heart, as you shook Dallas's hands and gave them fist bumps and hugs, you knew that once you left the court and headed to the locker room there would be no light at the end of the tunnel for a long time, only harsh criticism. Everyone just had to let it run its course until eventually the media daggers stopped piercing your psyche. Then, you could come back to life, accept the result, and change.

The Big Three changed voluntarily, accepting new roles. We were on our way back, knowing there would be another chance. If you care about changing and getting better, then you will sacrifice like you never have before. Everyone involved likes the fame, fortune, and recognition that sports success brings to someone involved with an NBA team at this level. Not everyone can accept the sacrifice necessary to achieve it. Your Miami Heat team did, and that feeling of deep misery would be dispelled. Sacrifice and trust were the antidotes.

Of all the changes that first Finals loss brought, the most important was clarity as to how LeBron's, Dwyane's, and your roles would evolve to help us avoid what happened in 2011. The player who sacrificed the most was you. You had always been the most talented player in Toronto—you led your team in every important statistical category. But the Raptors could not get to where you wanted them to be: playing for championships. Now, you fully and consciously embraced sacrificing your own statistics for the good of the team. In my opinion, you became the central figure in making this Big Three thing work. Your temperament, intelligence, and versatility turned us into a real monster. Not many superstars would become the third and sometimes fourth option. You did, and with that came championships. Over that summer of deep thought and tough discussions about roles and the addition of more depth, things changed for the better. There was less uncertainty about the machinations of the team a year later. The Heat matured big-time from the loss to Dallas, and this new Heat proved unstoppable. In the Finals, after a first game loss in OKC, we went on to win four straight games and celebrate the Big Three's first title at home. The championship quest was over. Five games and it was over. The rush of *knowing* what kind of team we had put together was pure. We had been contenders, and now we were champions. If we stayed together, we would be back to the Finals again and again. This monster of a team delivered. There were no tears of pain heading back to the locker room now, just euphoric screams, yelps, hugs, and glistening champagne running off your head into your eyes and creating the best tears: tears of joy. What a difference a year made.

## ADVERSITY

You were a young thirty-five years old and had not appeared in an NBA game since the 2015–16 season. The Miami Heat were honored to retire your number, jersey, and name on March 26, 2019, at American Airlines Arena, where you had performed with such greatness during your time with our team. There will be no player like you to ever run this floor again, ever—you were a unique person and performer. One of a kind. You were part of a great, great team from 2010–14: Four consecutive trips to the Finals and two world championships still stand as the greatest run in the history of the franchise. What a time of great basketball, great spirit, and rabid support from our fans and media. It was pure joy, made possible by a lot of togetherness. Winning does that. You could have played this game for twenty years if health issues had not cut short your career. In the summer of 2014, we lost LeBron, who decided to go back home to Cleveland. To say the least, we were all shocked and hurt by his decision, because after competing in four Finals and winning two world titles, we felt that the Big Three was just getting started on a dynastic run. But in spite of LeBron's leaving, we still felt the Heat was a great team with Dwyane and you as the focal points, with many productive, All Star–caliber years left between you. We just needed to surround you with very good complementary players that would make us competitive to chase titles. We became very aggressive, from the beginning of that off-season when LeBron left up to the trading deadline in February, in our efforts to upgrade the team. On February 19, 2015, at 6 p.m., we felt the acquisition of Goran Dragić from the Phoenix Suns could bring our team back on its way to title contention. Dragić was an aggressive all-around player, tough minded, and a fearless talent. He would be running alongside Dwyane in the backcourt. Just ten minutes after the trade was complete, a massive thunderbolt hit. I got a call from our doctor, who informed me that you would be sidelined for the rest of the season because of blood clot issues. I was stunned and very concerned about you and your overall health. We lost an irreplaceable talent, with numbers that could not be matched, and we lost a great leader, but at that point those things were irrelevant. The only concern was getting you back to great health. This was a devastating blow to you and the team. At first we thought the clotting issues would be resolved in time and you would be back the next year. In the meantime, while you were sidelined, we collapsed as a team. We were right there in playoff contention until early April, then we had a poor finish, and we failed to make the playoffs for the first time since 2008. Your loss was the main reason. It was just too much leadership and talent to lose.

In my fifty-three years of being involved with the NBA, this moment, of not knowing what your future would bring, was a true low point for me. There were many medical diagnoses of your condition, ranging from scary to terrifying. In this game, there are always basketball decisions and then there's the point where basketball becomes secondary to a player's health. Period. Over the next few years you did not play, as you worked relentlessly along with our organization to try to find remedies and protocols to allow you to get back on the court. At times this process became contentious. I had great compassion for you, Adrienne, and your family. To have someone tell you that your career is over because of a health condition is mind-boggling. But in all adversity, there is always a seed of equivalent benefit. I think you eventually found it in your family and friends, and in the realization that there was so much more that you could do with your life.

On that March day, when we raised your number 1 to the

rafters at the AAA, I was taken by all the people who showed complete love and respect for you and your family, as someone who had faced this great adversity and arrived at this point in his life able to say, It's OK, I have moved on. Your family, your friends, myself, and all your Heat family were in tears as we heard a man give the one thing we all wanted to hear. I loved being a Heat, you told us. I loved those championship runs. I loved you fans. You were a tower of power on that night, supremely gracious for all the good that had come to you in your life. At the end of your very poignant speech, your number now wafting in the rafters, you took the microphone out of its cradle and walked in front of the podium, up close to the fans, and shouted as loud as you could, just like you did after making a game-turning great play. With an abundance of enthusiasm, with that powerful voice, with your trademark Hulk-like pose, you yelled to everyone in the stands to be together with you one more time. COME ON, LET'S GO! . . . COME ON, LET'S GO! . . . COME ON, LET'S GO! . . . And we always did. You had your drop-the-mic moment right there. And yes, Chris, forever and for always, a HEAT LIFER you will be.

Love,

Pat

# LETTERS TO A
# YOUNG ATHLETE

# INTRODUCTION

The last thing you probably want is another voice in your head.

I get it.

There's a lot coming at you these days. Whether you're a once-in-a-lifetime talent just arriving in the pros, or an ordinary kid in an after-school league; whether you're playing basketball or lacrosse, throwing a shotput or suiting up as a tight end—or whether you're trying to excel in the classroom or start a career—you've got a *lot* of people coming at you.

Coaches.

Crushes.

Teammates.

Teachers.

Parents.

Peers.

The crowd.

There can also be recruiters, reporters, haters, and on and on. And then there's the toughest voice of all: the voice inside your own head. Nothing can intimidate you like that voice. Nothing can mislead you, shame you, puff you up, lead you astray, or keep you down quite like the running monologue between your own two ears.

But wherever they come from, all of those voices have something in common. Everybody *thinks* they know. They all want to tell you something—want to cop a few seconds to get in your ear. Or maybe they're firmer than that: *Sit your ass down, kid. You better listen to me.*

So here I am, another voice in your ear. What makes me any different?

Because I *know.* I don't just *think* I know. I've been there.

And where is "there"? It's where you are right now—high school, college, rookie—and where you want to go. I've been the kid in the driveway practicing buzzer-beaters and the guy in front of sold-out crowds hitting them, and neither all that long ago.

I remember what it was like to love the game. To break some kid's ankles on a crossover or drain a deep shot and realize, *Maybe I'm not like them. Maybe I've been given something special.* I remember what it was like to see that talent reflected back in the eyes of coaches and teammates, to realize that I had a future in basketball. I remember that hunger to make it, to get out of my hometown and *make it*. I remember being barraged by all the same people barraging you—about homework, about planning for the future, about sportsmanship, about being a team leader, about not hanging out with the wrong crowd, about trying hard, about the way you dress or the music you listen to, about everything that young athletes have always been hassled about.

I started playing baseball and basketball early. I was always tall. From maybe fourth grade on, basketball was more or less my life. I was Texas high school player of the year and an All-American before I was recruited by multiple colleges.

I've been there. I've been somewhere I imagine you want to go, even if it's the most unlikely of fantasies. I've heard thousands of people scream my name at once. I've been mobbed in the streets of foreign countries. I've run out of the tunnel onto an NBA court for a Game 7. I've *won* Game 7s. I've seen the confetti fall from the rafters. I played long enough to see my own jersey get raised up there, where it will hang forever.

I also avoided the trouble that a lot of athletes get into. I learned a lot about the game and about life. I know about heartbreak and pain, too. I made it to the pros and climbed to the very top of the profession I had worked my entire life to be a part of . . . only to suddenly lose it all when the thing that got me there—my body—betrayed me. A surprise blood clot in 2016 meant I would never again lace up my sneakers and play basketball in the NBA.

I was Bo Jackson, undone by a hip injury. I was Dajuan

Wagner, forced to retire early because of Crohn's disease. I was Jay Williams, severely injured in a motorcycle crash before his rookie year in the NBA. I was a million athletes you never heard of, because they were cut down before their prime. I was one of those athletes whose career didn't end soaked in champagne, celebrating a championship, or even in tears on the court. Instead, mine ended in a doctor's office in the middle of the afternoon. My playing days ended with a whimper, the slow drip of test results, doctors, and lawyers arguing over clauses in contracts over email.

As I write this, a part of me wishes I was still out there in the mix, chasing rings, but my dad always told me that when God closes a door, He opens a window. Our conversation here is a window for me. A window to explore the game from another angle and to give something back to the game that has given so much to me.

Believe me, I get that you probably don't want to listen to another person right now, but if you can make room for one more voice—for my voice—I think I can help you get where you want to go.

I've had lots of coaches. I've been lucky to play for some of the best—Erik Spoelstra, Coach K, Pat Riley, Mike D'Antoni. I've had coaches pull me aside and whisper exactly what I needed to hear at pivotal moments in a game, and in my life. I've had some pretty awful coaches in my life, too—the ones who don't have any motivational techniques beyond "yell louder" and "get more in their face." I've been screamed at by a lot of people. I tried to think about it the other day—the average attendance for an NBA game is about 18,000, and I played in 982 games in my NBA career. Add it all up, and that means I've had something like 17 *million* fans screaming at me *in person*—not to mention the millions more screaming at me through their TV.

The point is, I know about noise, and that's not what I'm going to throw at you.

There's too much at stake.

You see, you're at a crossroads in your life. You have two paths ahead of you, and you can only take one. I want to make sure you take the right one, the one that helps you get the most out of yourself, out of your potential, out of this game—whatever that game is for you. Whether you're staying at the gym hours after practice to work on your shot or cramming for an AP exam, I can help you get the most out of that.

Looking back, what really gives me vertigo is to think of those moments when I easily could have listened to the wrong voice. Where at fifteen, sixteen, seventeen, even twenty-seven, I could've messed things up forever with one wrong step. One moment of indulging the devil on my shoulder, and my life, my career, could have gone in a very different direction. My entire future—years in the pros, an Olympic gold medal, two championship rings—suddenly erased. And worse, like so many talented kids out there, I might never have even known what I had unwritten. Would I have my kids? Have my creativity? Would I even be here, alive? I was lucky in that way. I want you to be lucky, too.

One of the lucky moments for me was a conversation I still remember like yesterday. I was in high school, at the gym—I was always at the gym, I loved it—and my coach Thomas Hill asked me the kind of question most young kids never get, but almost always need.

Coach had been walking me through a drill. Maybe it was a low-post drill designed to teach the footwork for the jump hook, one of the most simple and devastating back-to-the-basket moves in all of basketball. They say you play like you practice, and for a low-post move like the jump hook to work, you've really got to commit, you've got to establish your position, get your footwork down, and get maximum arm extension to hopefully get you an easy two. Or maybe we were working on inbounding the ball and he was right up in my face, trying to flood me with pressure. Anyway, I must have been having a good workout because suddenly Coach Hill stopped everything, looked me in the eyes, and said, "What do you want to do with this, Chris?"

*What do I want to do with this? Man*, I thought, *I am doing this. Don't you see me playing?*

I stammered and stumbled a bit, thinking he wanted to hear about my goals for that very drill or maybe my goals for basketball. I explained I was maybe hoping to win a state championship or get a college scholarship, thinking that, of course, that's what every coach wants to hear. But he was thinking much bigger. He was thinking beyond the game. *Nah*, he said, *I'm talking more than that*. He wanted me to think bigger, too. What did I want to do with my life? Who did I want to be? How could basketball help me get there? Where could my talents take me and where could I go if I really sold that first step and put everything I had into driving toward my goals?

No matter what kind of talent you've been blessed with, you still have to answer the same question: What do you want to do with this? Where are you going, and how can you use what you've been given to get there?

That conversation changed my life, and a big reason I'm writing this book is that I want to ask the same question of you. However you answer it, answer it honestly—and I'll try to give you some honest advice about how I think you can get there. I don't want this to be just another noise in your ear—I want it to be one of the voices that matters. I want it to be like the conversations that helped me harness my talent, that helped me come to peace with the early end to my career. I want it to be like the conversations that happen between coaches and kids in locker rooms and in gyms, on buses to road games, and on the bench in the fourth quarter. The great coach John Wooden once said, "What you are as a person is far more important than what you are as a basketball player." And I've been fortunate to have been surrounded by countless coaches, mentors, and teammates who lived by those words.

You'll notice this book is called *Letters to a Young Athlete.* I'm writing it to you as a kind of letter. It's modeled on some of my favorite books, like *Letters to a Young Poet* and *Letters to a Young*

*Jazz Musician.* Those might seem like strange books for a basketball player to be reading, but I love learning—from anyone who can teach me. I hope I can share some of that love with you. I also hope I can pass along some of the timeless wisdom I've picked up along the way. One of the things the poet Rilke taught me is that part of being wise is accepting you don't have all of the answers right now—and that's OK. It's OK to be full of questions. "Try to love the questions themselves as if they were locked rooms or books written in a very foreign language," he wrote in *Letters to a Young Poet.* "Don't search for the answers, which could not be given to you now, because you would not be able to live them. And the point is, to live everything. Live the questions now. Perhaps then, someday far in the future, you will gradually, without even noticing it, live your way into the answer."

You don't have to know right now what you are going to do with the talent you've been given. You don't need to know where you're going to end up, or where you're going to find the strength you need along the way. Live, keep your love of the game close to you, and you can live yourself into the answers.

There isn't a roadmap to get you there, but Rilke's advice, which I've tried to take to heart, is that you have to *live everything.* What that means to me, as an athlete, is that your game—whatever it is—has to be more than a means to an end. Sure, you run the drills in practice because you want to win the games. You want to win the games because you want all of the good things that come with winning—trophies, pride, money, whatever. But if you don't stop to *live* what you're doing—if you don't make space to experience the joy of the game—you're missing something. You're missing the *biggest* thing.

And here's what's really special: You don't have to be a pro to experience those moments. There are plenty of pros who play the game mechanically and joylessly, and right now there's some kid shooting hoops at the local Y who could teach us all something about what it means to find joy in the game. Whatever our game of choice, whatever kind of talent we're blessed with, wherever we're hoping the game will take us, we're all the same when it comes to this: We all have that capacity to stop and experience the joy of what we're doing. As you'll see in these letters, that's gotten me through a lot of hard times. My wish for you is that when you look back on your playing days, you'll be able to say the same.

# WHEN YOU AIN'T NOTHING BUT TIRED

You're tired, yeah?

Welcome to the club.

Sometimes it feels like the primary sensation in an athlete's life isn't winning, or passion, or that amazing flow state when you *can't miss*—but exhaustion. You're just tired. All the time. Bone-ass exhausted.

Tired from practice. Tired from games. Tired from film study. Tired from school or work. Tired from it all, tired of all of it.

And maybe you're tired and you're not even through the second damn quarter—of the game, of your career, of your life. That wave of exhaustion doesn't care how much time is left on the clock. Once it gets its shoulders square and starts running downhill, it's coming for you like Marshawn Lynch through the

A-gap. But because there's still time on the clock, you've got to find—somehow, from somewhere—that extra bit of resolve, that last reserve of energy to withstand the blow and get you through.

How many times have you heard a coach telling you to give "110 percent" on the court, on the field, or in the weight room? Well, 110 percent is mathematically impossible. And there are times when finding that extra spark seems just as impossible. Then, somehow, you do.

You know who blew me away when it comes to that? Candace Parker, the WNBA champion power forward for the Los Angeles Sparks. She had a two-year stretch in 2008–09, right at the beginning of her career, that makes me feel like I was taking a nap that whole time. First, she leads the Tennessee Volunteers to the women's NCAA championship for the second year in a row. She wins Most Outstanding Player for the second year in a row. She gets drafted by the Sparks first overall in the WNBA draft *the next day*, flies out to Los Angeles for the press conference the day after that, and she's in her first professional game six weeks later. Then, two months later, in the middle of *that* season there's a break and she joins the U.S. women's Olympic team in Beijing and wins a gold medal. When that's over she comes back to the Sparks and finishes off that season, where she wins Rookie of the Year and Most Valuable Player. And if that's not already enough, she was planning on going overseas to play right after, but she couldn't because she got married and had a baby girl, and she only missed the first eight games of the next WNBA season.

"It was just kind of on to the next," she told me. "As a female basketball player you really don't have time to stop and smell the roses, because it's just grind after grind after grind after grind."

You can just *feel* the grind in her words. You can hear her body aching, you can feel the creak of her joints and the chill of the ice bath she's sliding into, if she even has the time between traveling for road trips, traveling overseas for the next season, and taking care of her kids. That's the life we signed up for, whatever sport we play. Candace played seven straight years of that crazy schedule, and it was the mental fatigue that ended up being the toughest opponent. "Just mentally trying to get yourself up for a regular-season game, knowing that you have so much basketball ahead of you—that's the toughest part," she said.

When I think about high school, one feeling comes to my mind first: dread. I remember literally *dreading* practice—it was so hard, and I was so tired. We had a coach my freshman year named Robert Allen, and I can still hear him blowing the whistle and saying, "Hey, we need to work on our conditioning." My heart would sink down into my shoes when I heard those words, man. Because I knew what it meant. I was going to have to push myself to sprint past the "E" on my tank, and I wasn't sure where that last bit of fuel was going to come from. I was going to experience pain and have to push through it over and over and would suffer worse consequences if I didn't run fast enough.

How did we get the strength to do it, when we just felt like we were *dying*? Maybe we knew that the other teams were out there doing it, too, and if we gave up they would run us off the court. You could say my teammates and I were trying to outrun that fear of losing. It's a healthy kind of fear if you keep it in perspective, which is a hard thing to do at that age.

Running those suicides. Running those drills over and over again, panting for breath, gasping from thirst. Running laps when you mess up. All you want is to catch your breath. Get a short break. Two minutes, one minute—hell, fifteen seconds— to catch your breath, and you know it just isn't coming. Ever.

Because as Candace said, it was on to the next. Grind after grind after grind.

Coach Allen was trying to break us. At least that's what it felt like at the time. He was also trying to teach us where to dig for that extra reserve of strength. To put it in more technical terms, he was helping us train our bodies to extract more oxygen from each breath. There's a reason that athletes have made sprints a part of their training since ancient times: Most sports—basketball included—involve a period of intense, maximum exertion, followed by a short pause, followed by another period of intense, maximum exertion. The ball gets inbounded, you race up the court to start the offense, miss a shot and race back on defense, then the whistle blows for a foul . . . if you're lucky. Playing basketball is doing some version of that pattern over and over again for forty-eight minutes. Sometimes the pattern repeats every twenty-four seconds, sometimes you're playing Mike D'Antoni's "seven seconds or less" Phoenix Suns and the pattern repeats more times than you can count. Wind sprints are basically that same pattern, stripped all the way down to the essentials. And if you want to get better at it, the only way is to practice it again and again.

What our coach wanted us to get better at—like any athlete in any sport—was playing well even when we were exhausted; getting good at hanging on to our desire to continue competing.

I'll start this book by telling you something I really believe: How an athlete plays when they're exhausted tells you everything about who they are as a competitor. The successful ones don't even think about being exhausted. They're so used to it that all they think about is performing.

In fact, maybe that's what being an athlete really is—enduring and transcending the limits you feel when, as The Boss once sang, you "ain't nothing but tired."

A couple of years into my career with the Toronto Raptors, I started hearing players from opposing teams ask me different versions of the same question when one of my teammates was at the foul line and we were standing on the lane lines waiting for that second free throw.

"What we gonna do here?"

"Yo, you going for it?"

At first I didn't understand what they were talking about. It sounded like something you'd hear from hockey players right before they dropped their gloves and squared up on each other. I looked at them, standing in the spaces closest to the rim, bent

LETTERS TO A YOUNG ATHLETE

forward at the waist, tugging at the legs of their shorts, trying to front for their coaches and for the cameras that they weren't gassed.

Then I got it.

They meant, *Was I going to try to get the rebound if my guy missed?* They wanted to make a gentlemen's agreement: Since the team on D would normally grab the rebound on a missed second free throw, by virtue of their superior position under the rim, I wouldn't make them work for it. If I agreed, neither of us would needlessly tire the other out—and the outcome would probably be the same anyway. If we could come to an understanding, it would save us both a pointless jump, without incurring the coach's wrath.

It was like the NBA bro-code. Or like two heavyweight boxers in the eighth round, wrapped up in the clinch, silently agreeing to and grateful for a few seconds' rest. Did I participate in that? I did. Players might claim they didn't, but we all did. But I do hope when you hear about that, you recoil a little.

Agreeing not to give your best—in any circumstance, for any reason—is cheating yourself. It's cheating the game. And yet as I got further into my career, I sometimes grabbed that rest like a thirsty man in the desert. I felt that mental fatigue Candace was talking about, and there were days when I gave in to it. Every big man has. Every *player* has in one way or another.

I hated the idea of quitting on a rebound opportunity, even when I was doing it. *Especially* then. I hated it, but I hate it even more now. If you want to be great, you're going to have to hate it, too.

You think Kobe Bryant just said all of a sudden, "Man I'm just really, really in shape, and now I can score 30 points a night without getting tired"? No way. You get that way by never quitting, by pushing through precisely when you are tired. That's the irony of this game: You become capable of the grind by surviving the grind.

My whole career I watched players like Kobe, Rip Hamilton, and Tim Duncan find that extra gear deep in the fourth quarter of games, from the best seat in the house—right on the court with them. Kobe toying with me when I picked him up on the switch in a high pick-and-roll. Duncan putting that big butt of his into my stomach and moving me, putting me on my heels, to set up his unstoppable turnaround off the glass. I remember realizing I couldn't keep up with him in the fourth quarter, and I remember the gut-wrenching pain of realizing that I didn't have what it took—yet. But *schooled* is the word—even on those nights when they beat me, they were teaching me, too. They were teaching me that the greats have another level.

I wanted to unlock that level. To gain that ability to play the way they played, dominating the game in the closing moments. We had a saying when I was growing up: You might as well bust your ass or get your ass busted.

Sure, it's easy to talk about how important practice is, and to nod your head when someone else says those words. But it's a lot harder when you're doing two-a-days in the Texas summer and you're still not getting playing time. It's hard on a fast break when you're the only guy back on defense and there's no way you're stopping anything. And it's hard 70 games into the season, and you know that you have a whole month of games left, none of which really matter because you're completely out of playoff contention, or your playoff berth is locked up and you just want to preserve your energy, and the guy next to you on the block asks if you're planning on going for the rebound. I remember that from my rookie year with Toronto. We were well out of the playoffs, and I was hurting from my first pro season, but I still took pride in going out there with two knee braces on and playing 35 or 40 minutes a night.

At moments like that, it's hard to push through. But I've always believed that how you do anything is how you do everything. If you make excuses or take shortcuts in one part of your life or your game, it's very hard not to do it everywhere else. If you take rebounds off when it doesn't matter, it's that much harder to find the will to crash the boards when it does. If you take a play off when you think no one is looking, where are you going to find the strength to keep going when it's the playoffs, when everyone is going 100 miles an hour, when your opponent wants that rebound just as much as you do?

I am fascinated with David Goggins, an ex–Navy SEAL who runs ultramarathons—the kind where you cover 135 miles in twenty-four hours. How does someone like that run for an entire day straight? David said that it's all about learning to distrust your limits: When you *think* you've hit your limit, you're only at about 40 percent of your capacity. Your mind is telling you that your body needs to stop—but it's lying. Your body can keep going well beyond that point. Realizing this should empower you. Imagine if a mechanic told you that your car's "Empty" light is malfunctioning, and when it comes on, you can still drive for another 200 miles. If that were the case, you'd stop paying attention to the Empty light until you could get it fixed. Well, I'm telling you from experience that your mental sense of your limits is just like that malfunctioning light: You can safely ignore it. The only difference is that there's no mechanic who can fix the light for you. It's still going to turn on when you have 200 miles' worth of gas in the tank—you just have to push yourself.

Whether it's a big game in Little League, or a challenge race for a spot on the relay team, or there's a loose ball on the court with a few seconds left on the shot clock, you've got to know that when you're tired and your mind tells you you ain't got nothing left, it's lying. Because it is. You are capable of more. We all are. Maybe the biggest difference between great athletes and mediocre ones is the learned ability to distrust that malfunctioning Empty light in their brains.

That's what pushing yourself in practice and in the gym is for. It's not just physical—it's mental. It teaches you about your Empty light, and when to ignore it. I remember the first time I ran a mile in practice. The whole time, I had that "little man" on my shoulder, telling me that there was no way, telling me that I was going to collapse before I made it a whole mile. And then I made it. I thought, *Damn, I pushed through that voice. I can do it. What else can I do?* If you're pushing yourself in practice, you're having a version of that thought every day. You aren't just teaching your lungs and heart to keep up with your legs—you're teaching yourself to beat that voice in your head.

Winning, or doing anything worthwhile, requires accessing materials or energies from deep within that are not typically accessed. It's just a fact. I've seen it my whole career.

One of the moments that defines my time with the Heat is that ball I kicked out to Ray Allen for the game-tying three in Game 6 of the 2013 Finals. Maybe you saw that on TV. A lot of people did. What they mostly saw is that I hustled to get the rebound, and then Ray hit the shot. What is easy to miss is the context that went into that hustle.

That was my 96th game of the season. We were six games into our series against the Spurs, and we'd gone seven games in the series before with the Pacers. I went up for the rebound in the 48th minute of a 48-minute game that then went into overtime. Next thing I knew I had to go up for the tip-off against the greatest power forward ever to play the game—Tim Duncan.

I don't know if I'm getting through to you how exhausted you can be after 96 games of NBA-level competition, against another team of competitors that is going just as hard. Take the most tired you've ever been and multiply it by about twenty. That's how tired.

Remember, no one is taking a play off. There's no bro-code with a series on the line, when a ring is in sight. At the highest levels, everyone going 100 miles per hour, and at the same time, everyone desperately wants to stop, and then there's a rebound and you have to sprint back on defense. And sometimes it's Russell Westbrook who got that rebound and he's coming at you like half cheetah and half water buffalo. This is when your body instinctively reacts to all the hurt it's feeling and your mind just has to tell it to shut up, which it does without consciously thinking—because if you did start consciously thinking, you'd realize that what you were doing was *insane*.

What Ray said about the ending to Game 6 has always stuck with me: Imagine if we put in just a little less in practice. Imagine if we coasted just a little bit more. Imagine we had a little less in the tank when it counted. "It would've been a shame for that to cost us a championship." But instead, we put in the work so we had what it took at the moment it was needed. By the time we got to that life-or-death situation, it was what Ray called "familiar territory." We knew what it was like to be playing on empty, so we could play on empty when it counted. And Ray, in particular, knew what it felt like to hit a game-winning shot from that spot on the floor, in that game situation, in front of eighteen thousand people—because he'd practiced it and envisioned it over and over. He practiced it when he was tired. He practiced it *after* practice. Which is how his whole body knew, really. His toes knew where the three-point line was. His heels knew where the sideline was. His quads and calves knew how much lift they needed to give him. His hands knew where they belonged on the ball. His elbow knew how to find his shooting pocket. They'd each been there hundreds of thousands of times.

Maybe you've watched a game like that Game 6 on TV. You see everyone soaked in sweat at the end, you see the winners celebrating and the losers hitting the showers, and maybe you imagine that, because these are pro athletes, everyone out there feels basically OK at the end. Maybe they're a bit winded, but not much the worse for wear, right?

No way. Everyone you're watching out there hurts. Everyone is in pain. Our reward for winning that toss-up against Tim Duncan was living to play another day in a Game 7 that promised to be harder than what we just experienced.

I still remember what our team president, Pat Riley, liked to say. "Scratch the depths of your soul and see what's there." Well, in that series, our team found out what was there.

No amount of work can make you taller. You can't make your hands bigger. You can work on your reaction time and reflexes, but to a certain extent they're just hardwired. But grit? Dedication? Learning to ignore that deceiving Empty light? That's on you. That's up to you.

Talent doesn't have anything to do with effort and conditioning. You don't have to be talented to be a well-conditioned athlete or a well-conditioned person. You don't have to have any talent or athletic ability at all to work out. I've seen so many guys do so much for themselves just by being in better condition than guys on the other team or guys they're competing against for a roster spot. It is grit and conditioning that gets them to the loose ball or the offensive rebound or to their spot on the floor, not talent. J. J. Redick is an incredible shooter, but he's been in the league more than fifteen years now because that dude does not stop running in the half-court. He would tell you that he doesn't have the athletic ability of 95 percent of the guys currently on an NBA roster, but he will run under, over, around, and through screens all day long until he pops free at a spot on the floor to let the one major talent advantage he does have—shooting—take over. That's what it's going to come down to sometimes. Sometimes it's going to be a marathon, other times just a bare-knuckle brawl. Sometimes the last man standing wins. Sometimes it's the last man moving.

Three of the toughest guys in the NBA when I was coming up were Dennis Rodman, Scottie Pippen, and Ben Wallace. They made their names on defense and on the boards. Want to know where they went to college? Southeastern Oklahoma State, Central Arkansas, and Virginia Union, respectively. They did not have the "talent" to attract scholarships to big-time D-1 programs. They only had grit and toughness and conditioning. You know what else they have in common? Fifteen-plus-year careers, and twelve rings between them. They're all champions.

Me? I went to Georgia Tech. It's a good school, but you know, it's no Duke or Kentucky. It was a less sexy path, but one I was confident in because I knew I was a *worker.*

If you can run for sixty minutes and still play defense at the end, that'll keep you in the conversation. On the other hand, if you spend all summer working on your ball handling and your shot, but you're not in shape, the only place you'll be in the conversation is in the comments section at the bottom of the You-Tube video you made in your driveway showing off your sick handle. Those skills won't mean anything in the real game when you're tired—you can just throw them out the door.

I hope this doesn't feel like the lecture of someone to whom all this came naturally, like when a morning person just says, "Oh yeah, wake up earlier!" As I said before, building endurance is hard. Almost never have I said, "Hey, man, I can't wait to do those sprints." To be honest, I have always *hated* running. Hated it. So I was scared. Scared of the exhaustion. Scared of not being able to catch my breath. Scared of the burning in my muscles. Scared of getting shown up by my teammates. Scared of getting called out by the coach for lagging. I used to dread practice because I knew these feelings were going to be inevitable.

And yet I kept doing it. I embraced that. And embracing that, it helped me get better. You know what I mean? It really, really helped me get better. I said to myself, I might as well get it over with. Because sometimes that's all you need to get through the next sprint, and the one after that. Sprinting up the court when your legs are on fire—it's just part of the job description of a basketball player. Your legs are gonna burn, your chest is gonna burn. You just have to get used to it—and you have to get used to the feeling of pushing through those limits.

In the off-seasons, I ran for miles with my trainer, Ken Roberson. He trained me, Larry Johnson, Kurt Thomas, LaMarcus Aldridge—a bunch of guys from Dallas. And we would run mile after mile, every day. Sub-six-minute miles. Every day. And one of the things that it taught us to do was to push through that fatigue. Continue to fight with that inner demon, that little voice, that little devil in your head telling you to stop—begging you to stop. "Please stop, just for a second. Please!"

But you find yourself getting used to that feeling. Getting used to those calves burning. Getting used to hearing that voice on the second or third lap and telling it to be quiet. That pain is temporary; championships are forever.

You have to figure out how to love it—all the sprints, all the miles, all the weights, all the preparation. Pretend you love it, trick yourself into loving it, whatever it takes. The difference between a runner-up and a champion is the difference between someone who says, "This is miserable—I quit," and someone who says, "This is miserable—give me more!" Or as Muhammad Ali put it: "I hated every minute of training, but I said, 'Don't quit. Suffer now and live the rest of your life as a champion.'"

Pain is temporary; glory is forever. If you want to excel, you have to get used to the pain. You have to get used to exhaustion. I can't promise you that it will ever be a comfortable feeling, but I can guarantee you that you can become familiar enough with it that you can visit that mental and physical space on your path to getting better and not have to worry that you'll crumple under the pressure.

You can't make that pain or exhaustion stop feeling like pain or exhaustion. But you can learn to welcome them in—to say, "Oh, I remember you. I know what this is going to be like."

So when you're sweating and panting in the last few minutes of the fourth quarter, and your heart's racing, you don't have to panic. You can say to yourself, "I've been here before." You want to be able to say, "I got this." You will be able to focus on the game and not those burning muscles.

It's there, at the outer limits of your endurance, where you find out what you're really made of. And when it's game time, that work pays off. Not just in the game, but everywhere. When you're running suicides in practice, it's over when the coach says it's over. But in the game, it's not over until there's zero on the clock and a winner has been decided. How often you end up on the winner's side of the final score is really up to you and how far you choose to push yourself.

And in life, it's the same. Life doesn't wait to see if you're rested and ready before throwing the biggest tests at you. It throws those tests at you whenever it feels like it—you lose your job, or you fail at something that mattered deeply to you, or someone you love gets really sick (just wait until you have kids!). The difference between people who crumple in the face of adversity and the people who come through it stronger and wiser is the ability to reach down for that extra endurance even when you're exhausted, even when it's not fair, even when you want to curl up in a hole somewhere. When times are hard, your mind may be telling you that you've hit your limit. Remember: It's lying.

So yeah, I get being tired. I empathize with it, I really do. I can almost feel you nodding off as you read this, on the team bus or in your bedroom after having done your homework and your chores and spent another long day in the weight room.

I feel that.

But you know what I say? I say *good*.

You're building your muscle. You're becoming stronger mentally, you're becoming more familiar with a kind of discomfort most people can't stand. You're building the strength that you're going to need when the game is on the line, when something really important is on the line. You're building *supreme conditioning*. The ability not just to keep going, but to *want* to keep going.

Your opponent is going to see this when you look them in the eye across the ball. They're not going to see anything but how straight you're standing and how they can't believe you still have anything left. Remember, the other guy is dead-ass tired, too. When they look in your eyes and see that you're ready to go another round—in that moment, their will to win will break. All that will be left will be mopping it up on the court.

I know that seems a long way off. Because right now, you're just tired. You've got however many games left. Or you've got a long way left to rehab from that injury. You've got a massive deficit to overcome in your GPA or a gap to cover in your SAT scores if you want to make it to this college or that one.

It's so much. You're so burned out. It's almost like hell.

I get it. But you know what they say? If you're going through hell, *keep going.*

That's how it goes with this phase of your game. You have to keep going. And know that what's coming out on the other side is a stronger, tougher, and harder-to-beat you.

## LETTER 2

# YOU HAVE TO FIND YOUR WHY (AND IT CAN'T BE FAME OR MONEY)

I told you before about the coach who pulled me aside in high school. *What do you want to do with this, Chris?* he asked me.

It was a good question, and it helped me steer the course of my life. He wanted to know the answer to a question so many coaches take for granted: What was I doing this for? Could I see beyond the next game, the next season, and really think about the role I wanted basketball to play in my life? Could I really look beyond the work I was putting into the game and think about the purpose I was putting all of it in for?

All of it. You know what I mean: Getting in reps in the weight room when your friends are partying. Waking up before dawn to run. Pushing through the criticism or the doubters. Getting back on the court after a full practice or a game, when all of your muscles are telling you to quit, and shooting a hundred more free throws. What is all of that for?

Maybe my coach could've put it like this: *Why are you doing this, Chris?* Why are you at practice right now? Why are you working so hard? Why are you committing to the life of an athlete? And don't just say, "To win the state championship," because you need to think bigger than that.

I want to ask you the same question: What is your "why"?

You are lucky to be where are right now, so early in your athletic career, whether it becomes an actual career or just a lifelong hobby. You still have time to figure out your why, and to live by it. Because, believe me, there's nothing sadder than watching someone going through the motions with no real idea about why they're doing it. Those people aren't living their own lives, their own dreams. At best, they're living someone else's. You still have time to do better.

So what is your why?

I've been around the game for most of my life, and you'd be surprised how many really talented people can't answer that question. They might look like they're in charge on the court, but inside, they're passive. They've let other people make up their whys for them. "My dad signed me up." "Coach said I'd make a good power forward." "I guess I was always good at it, so I kept doing it." You can spend your whole life living out someone else's goals and dreams for you without ever coming up with dreams of your own.

So, sure, listen to your coach when he tells you to run suicides. But don't listen when he or she tries to tell you what this game means to you. You gotta figure that out for yourself.

It can't just be that you're tall. It can't just be that someone signed you up for a sport because they thought it would be a good outlet for your energy or something to do after school. That's a great start, but I'm asking you to really think.

It can't be that your heroes got rich and famous playing the game. You need to go deeper.

"I'm doing this because I want to win basketball games."

*Why?*

"Because I want to win a championship."

*Why is that important to you?*

"Because then people will look up to me."

*Why is* that *important to you?*

You see what I mean? When you ask enough whys, it gets real deep, real quick. Beneath your reasons for hitting the gym at 7 a.m. on a Saturday, you'll find some idea of who you want to be in this world, of what really matters to you—if you dig deep enough.

In *Start with Why*, Simon Sinek argues that "clarity of why" is behind most of the biggest successes, whether in business or politics or culture. If you ask a leader from a successful company what they're ultimately selling, they won't name a product—they'll give you a "why," an intangible something that draws customers in. Apple isn't selling computers—it's the idea of "Think different." Southwest isn't selling airline tickets—it's selling the idea that travel and adventure can be for regular people, too. Disney isn't just making movies—it's telling stories, stories so vivid you want to experience them in every form possible. Me? I wasn't playing ball—I was trying to be the best version of myself I could possibly be. I was trying to realize my potential in life, and I carry that why with me to this day.

You aren't a company, but you have to think about your mission statement. Beneath all the outward signs of success, what's the motivating force that pushes you to give your all?

It can't be going pro. It can't be getting rich. It can't be getting your own shoe. I've had those things, and sure, they're fun—but they're not enough. As we've talked about, this journey you're on is really, really hard. It might seem like that pot of gold at the end of the rainbow is enough to keep you pushing on through the hardest parts of this journey—but it just isn't enough.

All the rewards of success aren't whys—they're more like hows. They're tools for getting you where you want to go, but they're not the destination.

What *is* a why? Knowing—not just thinking, but *knowing*—that you're making the most of your God-given talents. The joy of operating at the peak of your ability. The joy of being part of a team that runs like a well-oiled machine.

For me, a big part of my why was the squeak of shoes on the gym floor. I just love that sound. The actual smell of the gym. I love the sensation of straining my muscles and feeling the strength in them. It's trusting that your teammate is going to be where you think he's going to be when you whip him a pass—and then he is. It's the hand helping you up off the floor when you're down. It's the swish of the ball through the net, the anticipation surging through your body in the seconds before tip-off, the feeling of the blood pounding through your body as the seconds tick down in a close game.

I remember distinctly one day, when I was in the fourth grade at Hutchins Elementary, we were waiting to play organized basketball for the first time and I felt this intense excitement. I'd played the game before, obviously, but usually with my friends on the playground with no scoreboards. There was something in me that was just feeling, like, *Wow. Basketball.* I played my heart out during the game, and the next day, as we got ready to play again, I heard people saying, "Hey, Chris Bosh is good. Chris Bosh can play." Even one of the teachers had noticed. I was being *seen.* I was showing what I could do. It was just the perfect intersection of something I was good at and recognition and validation for the work I was putting in. A few weeks later, I started playing organized basketball. Word had spread and a coach sought me out.

I've been lining up to play ever since. For the love of it. For the opportunity to show what I can do. But as I said, it's deeper than that. What I began to understand later was that it wasn't about "attention," it was that I had capabilities and talents—like all kids do—and when I put in the effort to realize them, I could do incredible things. That to become who you are in sports, in life, in business is the loudest statement a person can make.

That's my why. It's me saying: This is who I am. This is what I can do with what God and my parents gave me. It's me challenging the other athletes on the court, on my team, asking them to show me what they can do. Together, we become the best we can be.

In 2019, the New Orleans Saints were having one of their best seasons ever. Their coach, Sean Payton, wanted to give his team a little extra motivation to get them over the finish line to a championship. At the start of the playoffs, he hired two armed guards, got his 2010 Lombardi Trophy off the shelf, stacked about $120,000 in crisp bills (the player bonus for the team that wins the Super Bowl), and walked it through the locker room after practice. "You want this?" he asked. He let it hang there. Then he said, "Then win three games," and walked out.

It was a pretty badass move, and it would've looked awesome in *Any Given Sunday.* There's something raw about stripping it all down to that—cash and trophies—and just putting it up there to be lusted after. But guess what? It didn't work. The Saints lost the NFC championship to the Rams.

Yes, the Saints got robbed by a terrible missed pass interference call. And yes, only in sports movies does the coach's locker room speech have the sole impact on whether or not the team wins. But this is my book, so I'm running with it. I'm not going to tell you that the Saints lost because Coach Payton used some poor motivation—but still, I think it's better to go deeper. Extra money and shiny hardware . . . every guy in that locker room already had more money than they ever grew up with, and they've won plenty of hardware over the years, or they wouldn't be in the NFL.

Years earlier, Coach Payton put together a different display, one that I think connects to a more meaningful and powerful why. To me, it is one of the most moving motivational moments in sports history. In 2006, after the devastation of Hurricane Katrina, the Saints were set to reopen the Superdome. Football writer Robert Mays described what Payton did to get his team ready:

> Three days before they were set to reopen the Super-dome against the Falcons on *Monday Night Football,* Payton famously brought his team to the stadium for the first time. The players gathered on the 50-yard line, and without a word, a video came onto the Jumbotron. Spliced with images of the devastation were clips from that preseason.

The players knew that they weren't just playing to win a football game—they were carrying the weight of a proud, beaten, resilient city on their backs. "It was a heavy, heavy, quiet moment," said linebacker Scott Fujita. Before kickoff, said fullback Mike Karney, "I remember looking over at the Falcons and just thinking, 'They want no part of this game.' We had already won the game. It's that simple."

The turning point of the game was a blocked punt by Steve Gleason, which has since been immortalized in a statue outside the Superdome. When you heard the sound of Gleason putting his body in front of that punt—man, you could just hear the *why*. It wasn't money. It wasn't a trophy. It was about the city. It was about the power of using the game to give people hope, to bring them together. That's a why that Gleason and the Saints have carried forward as they helped rebuild that city and today as Gleason heroically fights ALS.

I remember that blocked punt, even if I didn't remember whether or not the Saints won the game. (I just looked it up—they did.) But what matters is that what those players were playing for was way more important than a paycheck, a win, a line on the stat sheet. They weren't playing for themselves. In their first year back in the Superdome, the team hung a banner that read: "Our home. Our team. Be a Saint." It was that energy that propelled them to a Super Bowl just a few years later. I don't think anyone from New Orleans was thinking about their bonus checks when they went down to Miami for the Super Bowl.

I'm not saying you can't win with materialistic motives. Of course you can.

My dad had a conversation with me when I was twelve years old. He said to me, "Hey, look, I can't pay for college. I'll tell you that right now. You should keep playing basketball, that's great.

You can get a scholarship playing ball." I appreciated that honesty. It gave me clarity and it gave me a why. Part of why I played was to get that scholarship. He helped me see basketball as a way to do something. He was saying: I can see you love this game and you've loved it since you were a boy, and because of that love, it can help you get a scholarship and go to a good school.

I'm better for having that extra motivation, but I meant it when I said it was only *extra*. Need is necessary but not sufficient in this life. Proof? There are plenty of talented kids who had everything they needed to make it, who had every financial incentive in the world to make it . . . and for some reason could never be bothered to put in the work or care enough to get it. Every generation who's balled out at the Drew League in LA or at Rucker Park in New York or any playground in America has a story about a guy they played with who could have made it to the league, if only . . . Yeah, if only.

Fame? Popularity? Sure, those are fun, but they don't last, either. Here's an experiment. Look at this list of names and see how many you recognize: David Thompson, Kareem Adbul-Jabbar, Dennis Johnson, George McGinnis, Paul Westphal, Marques Johnson, Maurice Lucas, Walter David, Jack Sikma, Artis Gilmore, Otis Birdsong. Those were the NBA Western Conference All-Stars from 1979, the most famous and popular players in the league. Yeah, you probably know Kareem—but the rest of them? Their fame didn't even last thirty years.

Pull up a '90s hip-hop playlist from Spotify. How many of

those songs have you heard of? Tupac, maybe. Biggie, maybe. And the rest? Nope. The biggest names in music. People who won Grammys. Who had the world by the balls. Gone . . . and forgotten.

Speaking of '90s hip-hop, here's what Nas said about writing *Illmatic*, one of the albums from that era that did stand the test of time: "It was about bringing you inside my apartment. It wasn't about being a rap star; it was about anything other than. I want you to know who I am: What the streets taste like, feel like, smell like. What the cops talk like, walk like, think like. What crackheads do—I wanted you to smell it, feel it. It was important to me that I told the story that way because I thought that it wouldn't be told if I didn't tell it."

*It wouldn't be told if I didn't tell it.* Who knows if that's the attitude that made it possible for Nas to drop an all-time classic. The point is, he had a why—the kind of attitude that means it doesn't matter if your story becomes a classic, because it's your story, and you have to tell it. *If I didn't play, no one would play like me. If I didn't play, my teammates would be worse off.*

That's a why—an answer that works whether you're winning or losing. Besides, if you've ever seen a sports movie, you know that winning isn't guaranteed to solve your problems. Everyone roots for the Mighty Ducks, the Bad News Bears—the underdogs. If you want to win so you'll be liked, you may end up surprised—you might end up getting just the opposite. Being the "favorite" doesn't always make you the fan favorite. In fact, we love rooting for people to fail!

And even if money and fame and popularity *were* good short-term motivators, what do you think is going to happen when you get them? Even rookie contracts are often life-changing money, but the best players keep going. Serena Williams will never have to work another minute in her life, and yet she is working every day; not just on her game, not just on her body, but on multiple companies she owns. Serena had more money than she could ever need, plus twenty-three Grand Slam titles, second most of all time. She then came back after her pregnancy to continue being one of the top players in tennis. Why? Because she has a much bigger *why* than living that life.

One of the more common whys I see—and it's one I sympathize with—is the drive to prove people wrong. Or to prove to the world that you matter, that you didn't deserve what happened to you early in life, that you were more than just where you came from, that the haters need to sit down. There's a part of all of us that uses success in sports to keep from ever feeling small. If you have self-esteem issues, or if you came from a broken home, the roar of the crowd can be a kind of substitute love. A basketball court can be like a home where you feel valued.

My first year with the Heat, the whole season long, I just wanted to shove our success in the face of everyone who criticized us. If I could just win this championship, I thought, I could shut the haters up. If I won, it'd make me feel better, right? Then I'd be just like the haters. I just wanted to prove them wrong.

That whole season, I never imagined losing. I just imagined shutting the haters up. You don't work for a whole season, fight all the way through the playoffs to the Finals, and really imagine that you're ever going to lose. It just doesn't enter your mind.

And suddenly there I was, at the end of the Finals, with the Mavericks celebrating on our court. My good friend Tyson Chandler encouraging me to keep my head up. It hit me: *This isn't going to have a happy ending. You're not shutting anyone up. You lost.*

You never really forget a loss like that, even if you win it all the next time, like we did. And in the weeks after we lost, I had a lot of time to sit with it. I don't think we lost because we had the wrong attitude about winning—we lost because we got outplayed. But in those weeks after the Finals, I imagined what it would have felt like to win with that attitude, to actually shut up the haters. Maybe you'll call it sour grapes, but I came to realize that winning like that wouldn't really make me happy. Maybe for a few days, or a few months. But not in the long run. Because my story would have been about the haters, not about what I accomplished with my teammates. Even if I won that way, I still would've been giving the haters power over me.

Victory gets old and unsatisfying really fast without a purpose you can be proud of. If you make anger your why, it will suck the joy out of everything you accomplish—even if you win as much as Jordan.

But here's the thing about a good why: It can endure through the ups and downs of life, even when everything around you is falling apart. Your what can be taken away from you in an instant—your why can outlast that.

Ryan Shazier was playing for the Pittsburgh Steelers—and then, boom, one hit took away his ability to walk. In 1949, there was a baseball player for the Phillies named Eddie Waitkus. He was sitting in the team hotel when he got a call from the front desk saying that a former classmate was at the hotel and urgently needed him to come to her room. He walked over . . . and this mentally ill woman shot him in the chest with a .22 caliber rifle. He nearly died. Think of Bobby Hurley—he was a two-time college champion for Duke, Most Outstanding Player of the Final Four, bound for success in the pros, and as he was on his way home from a game in his rookie NBA season, his SUV was T-boned by a station wagon. Hurley was thrown from the wreck and nearly died.

When I think of Bobby Hurley, who is now the head coach at Arizona State, or Waitkus, who became Comeback Player of the Year, or Ryan Shazier, who has fought his way back to walking again, inch by inch, I see guys who clearly had a deeper why than just the superficial stuff. They had to. When someone like Hurley makes it back to basketball after life-threatening injuries, that's inspiring. But what's more inspiring to me is to know that even if he didn't make it back, he still would have found a way to live a life of meaning and purpose.

When I saw Zion Williamson go down in that freak accident in college when his shoe blew out, I had a flashback. What if it all came crumbling down for him? Fortunately, the injury wasn't nearly as bad as it looked. But what if it had been? What if he suddenly wasn't Zion, the most dominant player in college ball, the No. 1 pick in the NBA draft? Would he be able to handle that? Would he understand that there was life beyond and besides basketball? Or that there were other ways to benefit from the game besides being the star?

At that moment, I hoped he had someone in his life who did for him what Coach Hill did for me, when he asked me what I wanted to do with the game. Every young athlete needs to have that conversation, if not with a coach then with themselves. That's why I am asking you to start thinking about it: What are you playing for? What do you want to accomplish with the game? Through it? What doors do you want it to open? Who do you want to be on the court? In life?

Just like hauling yourself out of bed for extra practice, even when no one's making you—you have to use that same discipline to work on your why. You can try the exercise I mentioned at the beginning of this letter: starting with your superficial goals and asking "Why?" for each one, pushing yourself to go deeper and deeper into your real motivations. You might be surprised what you find. Maybe there's a spiritual or philosophical tradition that gives you a sense of what a purposeful life looks like—your game can be part of that. Or maybe it's more intuitive. Maybe there's a moment in the flow of a game when you stop for just half a second and think, *This right here—this is why I love this game.* You can feel your way toward your why.

And of course, you're growing and changing as you play the

game, and it's fine for your why to change as you grow. Hopefully, it'll get deeper and more mature as you get deeper and more mature. Before I developed a real love of the game—the kind of love that can sustain you through injury, adversity, and failure—I just wanted to spend time with my friends on the playground, shooting hoops. Whys change and evolve, just like people do. The key is to never invest your why in something external that can be taken away by a power beyond your control.

It has to be deeper than winning and losing, or getting some free money to pay for college. It's got to connect to your soul. It's got to connect you to something bigger than yourself.

It can't be about the hardware. It's got to be something hardwired, something infused in your DNA.

If you have that? It'll be like Mike Karney said. No opponent, no obstacle will want any part of you. You'll be unstoppable.

# LETTER 3

## THE GIFT OF HUNGER

O ne day, an NBA teammate of mine brought his son to get some shots up with the team before practice. I could tell right away that this kid, who was about high school age at the time, had serious talent. He also had a serious talent for talking smack—telling me he was gonna dunk on me and all that—but I respected that he was a competitor.

I could tell he wanted to win, that he'd put in the work. Clearly, his game reflected it. But what was driving his drive?

We just talked about your *why*. Maybe his was impressing his dad. Or mastering the game. Or making it to the league.

We talked about what drives you *when you ain't nothing but tired*. That's from Springsteen. Bruce Springsteen was a kid who came from nothing special, but like you wanted desperately to do something with his life. He ached to get out of his small town and make his mark on the world. He's called The Boss now for a reason, because he did it, and I'll quote him again, because he talked about what it takes to do this.

*Stay on the streets of this town*
*and they'll be carving you up alright*
*They say you gotta stay hungry*
*hey baby I'm just about starving tonight*

I'll tell you, though, when I was in high school, it was the comfortable, even spoiled kids that we carved right up. We ate their lunch up and down the court. Because for all their natural gifts, all their top-flight training and facilities, we had something that's really hard to manufacture. *We had real hunger.*

To be great, you have to be hungry. You have to *stay* hungry.

When it comes down to pulling in that last defensive rebound after you've been sprinting up and down the court for the better part of an hour, winning *has* to mean something. When it's crunch time, when your body is screaming at you to stop pushing, the pain of losing has to be greater than the pain of crashing the boards or diving for a loose ball one more time. That's hunger. When you think about the greats who can feel the pain of losing, or the joy of winning, so deep in their gut that it's almost a physical sensation, realize that their hunger is just as important to their success as their height or their lung capacity or their 40 time or their why.

You know how sportscasters wrap up a game and say something like, "Well, Jim, that team just wanted it more." I know—it's a huge cliché, right up there with "The team that scores the most points is going to win." Who doesn't want to win? But like most clichés, there's some truth in it.

Basketball isn't like the Hunger Games or the Roman Colosseum—nothing really *bad* happens to the losers outside of losing the game and any potential injuries. Especially in the pros, pretty much every player, winners and losers alike, is going to get into a fancy car at the end of the game, have a great dinner, and go to sleep in a comfy bed. And when your life looks like that, it's easy to tell yourself, "It's just a game. Win some, lose some." It's the players who ignore that—who know it's a game but still treat it like life or death for 48 minutes—who really do want it more. And yeah, over the course of a season, those players and those teams really do win some games that they should have lost. Hunger can't make you seven feet tall or tell you how to defend Steph Curry. But on those nights when your shot isn't falling, when you can't get a single call from the refs, when it seems like all the breaks are going against you, hunger can pull you through.

"That team just wanted it more" may be a cliché, but it's just a fact that not everyone on the court or the field wants to win with the same intensity. Even pros let up sometimes. A couple of years ago in a baseball game, there was a guy who hit a deep fly ball to right field in the seventh inning. He thought it was out of the park, so he stopped to admire his shot instead of running out of the batter's box. But the ball was just short of a homer, and because he had lagged, he had to settle for a single instead of a double. The team lost the game by a single run.

It's the type of scene that's happened a thousand times in a thousand games in every sport you can imagine. Even at the elite level, hunger is rarer than you think.

Still, they're different gifts. Just as lots of physically talented athletes don't have the same level of hunger, you don't have to be talented to play hungry. And film doesn't lie in that regard. You can see what I mean when you watch the NCAA tournament, where lots of lower seeds don't have rosters full of elite athletes, or even in "garbage time" of an NBA game. You can tell which players on the court have elite hunger, and which don't. The ones that do are all over the court, rebounding, going after every loose ball, playing until the whistle every time. They're playing hard even when the game is out of reach or put away, whether they're down 20 or up 20.

You can talk to any NBA player and they'll tell you about someone they knew who had all the talent he needed to be in the league, but just didn't have the drive. I've seen it—they'll tell you about the time he threw down a huge dunk or that epic game she took over in the fourth quarter, and they'll say something like, "He could've been great. He just . . ." And they'll trail off. But what they're saying is that, in a league full of elite talent, elite talent isn't enough.

I've seen too many people stop, get satisfied with making

varsity, with signing their first contract, or their first start, or their first shoe deal—and just lose the hunger (again, that's why money or recognition is a bad *why*). It's fine to celebrate. There's nothing like celebrating a win or a big moment. But some people just get stuck there. And meanwhile, life keeps going—other players are hitting the gym, new kids are coming up to the league from college, you're getting older, and your body is just a fraction less capable than it was the day before. Without hunger, life leaves you behind.

When I think about what made my career a success, I think the gift of hunger was a big part of it. I didn't have it as bad as some kids did when I was coming up. I was blessed to be able to work out at a high school gym with some basic hand-me-down weight machines, even if there was nothing fancy. But when my teammates and I went up against kids from better-off schools, kids who had the resources we never got, we loved it. We feasted on that kind of competition. I remember thinking, *At the end of this game, I'm gonna go back to my life, and you're gonna go back to yours, and there's gonna be a huge difference. But right now, on this court, we're equals. Right now I want this in a way that you can't even understand.*

Maybe you come from something like my situation, or something much worse. And while it's foolish to imagine that basketball or some other sport is a guaranteed ticket to a better life—for the vast majority of young players, it isn't—I want you to understand that hunger is a gift. At the end of the day, hunger is a lot more about showing that you can compete on equal terms with anyone on any given day. Hunger is what makes Draymond Green great. It's what made him the most important player on a championship team. He just wants it more than most guys, because he never had "it" like most of them going into or coming out of college.

Of course, some of the young athletes reading this book will be a lot more comfortable than I was growing up. That doesn't mean that they can't make it to the highest levels—look at someone like Klay Thompson, Draymond's teammate, or Austin Rivers, or Tim Hardaway Jr., whose dads were NBA stars before them. All four of Rick Barry's boys made it to the league. Look at Steph and Seth Curry.

So it's not just about money or resources. Maybe part of what drove them was proving that they *weren't* just good because of their dads. That having a nice car didn't say anything about them, but *this dunk does*.

Hunger will be the difference maker. Michael Jordan knows it. He told the Bulls before that series when they finally got over the Detroit Pistons, "Even though they may have that experience, we have that hunger."

In an even match, or maybe even in a totally lopsided contest, hunger is the swing vote.

Lewis Hamilton reports to Formula 1 every year focused and ready to go despite having seven world championships. He's the best driver in the world and his hunger keeps him getting better so that he can continue to perform at the highest level. And this is in a sport where being off your game can make the difference between life and death. He changed his diet and physio routine so that he can perform and focus better while he's on the track. He needed it to win his third consecutive title that's still active as I write this. He's tied with the all-time record held by Michael Schumacher.

After our first championship with the Heat, a friend told me, "Man, anybody can do it once. You gotta do it twice." Finding a reason for hunger when you have every reason to feel full—that's what separates good from great.

What keeps a guy like Tom Brady coming back? The same thing that keeps James Harden working on new shots in the off-season. What keeps a team like the Heat pushing for a second title when they could just sit back and enjoy the first one? The same thing that keeps writers writing, even after they've got a classic to their name. What keeps Elon Musk at it, starting new companies? It's not the financial rewards. It's just the joy of getting better, of wanting to beat your own personal best every time you lace up your shoes or step into your office. And it's *purpose*. For someone like Musk, it's about building technology that can keep human life sustainable on this planet, and someday on other planets, too. For someone like Brady, it's being remembered as the best to ever play the game. And that's something all of the greats have in common. They come in all kinds of body types, with all kinds of skill sets—but where the good ones stop, the great ones keep going. They're never satisfied. They're never full.

When you're lucky enough to play next to someone like that—like I was lucky enough to play next to LeBron James—you realize that they have every reason in the world to be arrogant, to think they're bigger than the game, and yet they're not like that at all. Part of their hunger is knowing that they can't cheat the game. Players like that never take a play or a practice off, and most of the time, they know and revere the game's history. They're leaders in practice even when they don't feel like it, even when the coach is getting on their last nerve. Their hunger gets them through those tough days. They respect the game too much to take it lightly. I watched LeBron play hungry every game, every practice.

And, of course, I grew up watching MJ do the same thing. Just like Brady, he could have easily rested on his laurels way before he retired. Pretty much any given night in the '90s, he could have said, "I'm Michael Jordan. Everyone knows what I can do. I'm gonna take it easy tonight." But he never did that—even when it took making up grudges and slights to give himself a reason to play hard every night. Someone with Jordan-level talent but not Jordan-level hunger might've been content with *one* championship. It takes both to get six.

And if you find ways to develop your gift of hunger, if you have teammates and coaches who inspire you to keep pushing, you find that hunger can become part of your life. It's like a virtuous cycle—the more work you put in, the hungrier you get, the harder you work, the hungrier you get, the more success you see, the hungrier you get.

But you do have to look for things to be hungry for, I think. You gotta work up that appetite; it doesn't come naturally. From what I've heard, this is something Bill Belichick is really good at. After he won that first Super Bowl, as the team was celebrating on the field, one of his scouts, so happy he had tears in his eyes, said, "What do we do now?" Belichick looked at him and said, "We win more!"

You can imagine it's been tough over the years to keep himself and his team motivated as the wins have piled up, but he's always been good at looking for slights. Oh, the media is out to get us, he'll tell the team. *They* don't think we can do it. What do these guys think, he'll say about the game next week, that they can come into our house and push us around? The mind of champion is like that. Otherwise, you stop being a champion.

I remember in high school being in a tournament where I set my mind on winning the MVP trophy. My eyes on that prize, I just about killed myself working for it. I was starving for it. You can imagine how it tasted when I got it. But as we were leaving, I heard some guys from another school called South Oak Cliff, a team who we didn't play, say, "Yo, why don't you give that trophy to somebody who deserves it?"

Man, that didn't feel good, but in retrospect, it was just about the greatest gift they could have given me. Because instead of rest-ing on my success, I got back in the gym *hard*. It was like it took me back to zero and reset me. I was going to come back the next year and beat them . . . and shut them up. That's exactly what we did. We beat them by 40 points my senior year to advance to the state final four. We just mopped the floor with them.

Little things like that fuel you. That hunger sustained me for years. I never forgot it. I never forget any of that stuff.

Even when my early hunger as a player got satisfied, what helped me go from high school to college then college to the pros then Toronto to Miami and then keep fighting for my spot, even when I was hurt or sick, was that I was always looking for new challenges. It's like a great chef: They've cooked the same dish night in and night out thousands of times, but they're always trying to cook it even better the next time, and make it taste better in the process. They've got that big hunger that's deeper than food.

Same goes for entrepreneurs. Michael Lewis said that they're always chasing the "new new thing," and I think that's a beautiful phrase. They want to know what's behind the mountains and then behind those mountains. You'll have to do that, too . . . unless your goal is to be average or to pull up and stop early.

At the same time, there are a lot of fables in history about those with insatiable appetites. You don't want to overreach and you don't want the joy of victory to become ash in your mouth.

Life keeps moving, and even hunger—as much as it makes the difference between the merely good and the truly great—can get out of control. Get *too* hungry and you can end up eating yourself—obsessing over games that ended years ago, beating yourself up over mistakes from the past, risking your health and your body when you need time to recover and heal. And just as I've seen talented players without enough hunger to excel, I've seen players hungry for the wrong things—for stats but not for winning, for ego gratification but not team success, for money but not joy in playing the game. I've talked a lot in this letter about staying hungry. But remember, *what* you're hungry for matters, too. That's why letting yourself be motivated and inspired by teammates and coaches makes such a difference. I talked about LeBron, and how his hunger is tied so closely to his love and respect for the game. Whenever he does hang it up, I'm sure he'll feel the sadness of that moment, but I'm also sure he'll be able to move on—because his hunger is for the right things, and because he knows that the game is bigger than any one of us.

# LETTER 4

## CULTIVATING THE MIND

One of the reasons I know you're going to be OK is because you're reading this. Or rather, you're *still* reading this.

Because you've made it through all these pages so far, and we haven't spent a single minute discussing how to cut into the lane, or how to position yourself for a rebound, or my favorite weight-lifting strategies.

This isn't that kind of book.

For some athletes, that would mean "Not interested."

I've heard this from coaches, too. Reading? Every minute spent reading is a minute you could spend watching film, or hitting the gym, or putting up a hundred more free throws. I've heard them say with pride, "I haven't read a book in years."

I remember when I joined the Heat, Spo had done his

research on me and he'd heard I was a reader, so he bought me a book he thought I would like and get something out of. He was always doing that for players. He got me *Outliers* by Malcolm Gladwell. When Spo handed it to me, I was touched, but it was funny because I had to tell him I'd already read it and loved it.

He looked at me like I had two heads.

Spo had been giving books to players for years and that had *never* happened before.

So I love that you are here right now, this early in life, putting work into your mental game. Trying to get better as a thinker, as a person, as a *whole package.* Sure, film and weights and free throws matter. But if you neglect the part of your body between your ears, there's always going to be a huge hole in your game, no matter what your sport is—because that part of your body is where the playbook and the film study go. My grandfather Daddy Jack was known for saying, "Use that thing in between your ears because if you don't, no one else will." You could be the biggest, baddest, fastest, hungriest person on the hardwood, but if you can't remember your defensive rotations or the tendencies of your man off the bounce versus when he's moving without the ball, you're going to be a liability out there.

I've been lucky enough that making a few bucks a copy is not something I care about much anymore (and if it was my motivation, that'd be a bad *why*, right?), so whether someone bought you this copy, or you got this from the library, or you're listening to some pirated audiobook version on YouTube, or if you're borrowing a dog-eared copy from a friend, I'm happy.

I am happy because you're reading. Because you *chose* to read.

It's some lame stereotype, probably from my parents' generation, that athletes are stupid jocks. Are there dumb athletes out there? Of course. There are not-very-bright plumbers and presidents, too, but the vast majority of athletes I've met—the really great ones—were more than just physically brilliant. You have to have an elite mind to be an elite player.

Aaron Rodgers, the quarterback for the Green Bay Packers, can famously recall plays, line protections, audibles, and decisions made by his receivers on individual plays in the middle of a game from five or six years ago. Even crazier, he knows what his receivers and backs *should* have been doing or what the play design *planned* for them to be doing, and how the defense moved to force them to check down or check with him for secondary routes. Interviewers' jaws drop when they test him on stuff like that, and they seem to be equally shocked when LeBron shows off his photographic memory at postgame press conferences, where he explains every single turnover he committed during a game, including details of who was guarding who and how he lost the ball. Really, it shouldn't be all that surprising—your mind is a part of your body, and you can and should take care of both at the same time. Honestly, it would be more surprising if someone like Rodgers or LeBron was a "dumb jock." How could someone read a defense in a half-second, anticipate his opponents' reactions, and then react *to* those reactions without having elite intelligence?

Or think about Greg Maddux. He was one of the most dominant pitchers when I was growing up. If you ever saw him pitch, you know he was pretty much untouchable in his prime. You also know that the dude looked like an accountant or a middle school teacher. He didn't have the dominating physical presence of a Randy Johnson or Roger Clemens. His fastball rarely got above 90 miles per hour. But he ended his career in the top ten all-time for strikeouts and wins—and he played right through baseball's steroid era and home-run explosion. It wasn't physical prowess that gave Maddux his edge. It was his mental advantage. He knew every single hitter's tendencies and weaknesses, he knew how they hit against him and even how he'd pitched them the last time they faced each other. Like a chess grand master, he'd played out at-bats before the game even started. He'd beaten 80 percent of the hitters he faced with his mind—with his focus and preparation and understanding of the game—before they'd even stepped into the batter's box.

There are tons of stories about Maddux's Jedi-level mental powers. Here's one from *Sports Illustrated* in 2004: "Once while seated in the Braves' dugout as third baseman Jose Hernandez batted for the Los Angeles Dodgers, Maddux blurted out, 'Watch this. The first base coach may be going to the hospital.' On the next pitch Hernandez drilled a line drive off the chest of the first base coach." To get a prediction like that right, you have to know what kind of pitch is coming given the game situation, how the hitter is going to react to it, and what's going to happen when he does. You have to understand physics at an intuitive level that would impress a Caltech professor.

I want you to develop that kind of mind.

The good news is you are on a track to make that happen. Take Richard Sherman. I always love when he points out that he went to Stanford. He's a legit scholar. He gave a speech a while back about his experience in college, and about all the parts of the student-athlete life you don't see on TV. When the NCAA tries to explain why college athletes don't get paid, Sherman said, it points out that they get free scholarships. But, as Sherman explained, what the NCAA doesn't talk about is how insanely difficult it is to balance education and athletics:

> I would love for a regular student to have a student-athlete's schedule during the season for just one quarter or one semester and show me how you balance that. Show me how you would schedule your classes when you can't schedule classes from two to six o'clock on any given day. Show me how you're going to get all your work done when after you get out at seven-thirty or so, you've got a test the next day, you're dead tired from practice and you still have to study just as hard as everybody else every day and get all the same work done . . .

You wake up in the morning, you have weights at this time. Then after weights you go to class, and after class, you go maybe try to grab you a quick bite to eat. Then after you get your quick bite to eat, you go straight to meetings, and after meetings, you've got practice, and after practice, you've got to try to get all the work done you had throughout the day you've got from your lectures.

You can be a student-athlete like that. Even if you've already graduated. It's just something you have to commit to. Getting smart is not an accident, just like getting strong isn't one either. Richard Sherman put in the work on his mind and his body. So should you.

Whenever I see young athletes neglecting their studies because they're so confident they're going to make bank in the pros, it just looks to me like they're shooting themselves in the foot. Sure, no one's going to decide the state basketball championship by assigning a geometry test at half-court. But so much of success at the game depends on mental sharpness, mental recall, mental creativity, mental resilience, mental preparedness, and, yes, even some intuitive geometry.

When guys like Kevin Love throw one of those crazy full-court outlet passes off a missed shot, it's always from the perfect angle so that the outlet guy can catch it in stride and put it right up, and so his chase defender can't just stick his hand up and bat it away. It's the same for quarterbacks on slant routes and deep crosses; for pool players on long bank shots; for soccer players on corner kicks; and for hockey players passing the puck on a break into the offensive zone. It's all real-time geometry.

So whenever anyone says that working on your mind is a distraction from working on your game, I think they've gotten it completely backward. Most game nights, I made sure to take some time to read a book before suiting up. I learned that I was only going to be able to play at my best if I could stay mentally sharp, so that meant exercising my mind along with my body.

And the fact that you're reading this book tells me that you get it. Of course, it didn't have to be *this* book—it's just that you've decided to spend some time doing something more demanding for your mind than picking up a video game or scrolling through Instagram. Don't let anyone tell you that reading books, thinking hard, pushing your mind isn't for athletes. Those things are a crucial part of your success—during your athletic career and afterward. Because unless something tragic happens, there's going to be an afterward, and what you do to cultivate your mind right now will make the difference between your afterward being a rewarding part of your journey and being a boring slog.

*Cultivate* your mind. If you didn't know where that word comes from, it comes from a Latin word that means "to grow," like how you cultivate a garden or a piece of farmland. Cultivation isn't something that happens overnight. It's a long, patient, methodical process. You have to plant the seeds—that's learning the basics, figuring out what you're passionate about outside of your sport, paying attention in class. You have to water the seeds—that's coming back to the thing you're passionate about almost every day, putting in the time, developing your mastery. And then you get to collect the fruit, your reward for all of that work. In this case, the reward is that you get to be an interesting person—to others, sure, but mainly to yourself. You get to be the kind of person with something more than X's and O's bouncing around in your brain to keep you company.

Are you watching lots of game tape? Great. But that's not enough. The human brain is remarkably flexible—qualities that you build in one area of your mental life can transfer to others. So if you take an afternoon to read a novel, or go to a museum, or listen to a concert, or learn to cook a new recipe, that's not taking away from your game. That's transferring creativity, patience, and focus straight to your game, in a way that I promise will pay off. Your brain isn't literally a muscle, but it acts like a muscle in ways that an athlete will immediately recognize. When you're pushing it beyond its limits, it "hurts"—it's a struggle to build up your mind, just like it is to build up your muscles. When it recovers, you'll be surprised at how easily you can "lift" ideas and concepts that used to be beyond you. And if you slack off for a few days, your brain doesn't stay the way you left it. It's either getting stronger or getting weaker—every day. Just like your muscles.

In my experience, the best evidence of the way that expanding your mind transfers to athletics has to do with visualization. Whenever I'd read in school, I'd work on visualizing the stories and the characters in my head. I could see Harry Potter and his friends going to Hogwarts for another semester to learn magic. I liked that image of the green light across the water in *The Great Gatsby*. And I found that the more practice I got with that, the better I was able to visualize what happened on the court—whether it was replaying key moments from a game after they'd happened, or anticipating what was going to happen next. There isn't a part of my brain marked "basketball visualization" and "visualization for everything else." There's one part of my brain that's for visualization—and the more I strengthened it in the classroom, the more it helped me on the court.

For all the problems in the way college athletics is managed in this country, the basic idea of combining sports and academics is a really wise one. In Europe, they don't have that. You either go pro or you go to school. There is no real in-between. I think that's a shame. Sure, you end up with lots of athletes who focus on nothing but their game from a young age. But you also miss out on the kind of athletes that a college education at least has a chance of producing: athletes who understand the power structures that govern their sport and their society, who can advocate for themselves, who can be vocal about things that matter off the court. I'm sure there are athletes in the European system who can do those things, too. But there's something powerful about the ideal we have on this side of the pond—that being an athlete means training your brain as well as your body—no matter how bad we often are at living up to it.

Besides, the idea that you can cultivate *just* your body, or *just* your mind, is a really new and untested one in the scheme of things. For most of human history, we believed that your brain and your body were the same thing. You can't fully develop one without developing the other. There's even a Latin saying, *Mens sana in corpore sano*, which means "a sound mind in a sound body." It's been around for thousands of years. In the ancient world, being an educated person meant you knew things like geometry, poetry, and music—and it also meant that you knew how to do things like wrestle, throw a javelin, and run a footrace.

When I see athletes who think they can reach the height of their sport while leaving their minds behind—without cultivating their visualization skills, their memory, their creativity in the same way they build their muscles—they're kidding themselves. Especially these days, when data and analytics have taken over the game. Maybe you used to be able to get away with just being a genetic freak, but not anymore. If you've ever watched Giannis Antetokounmpo play, you know what I mean. Every shot he takes is either from in the paint or right at the rim. That's not a quirk—he's doing that because the analytics tell him (they tell everyone in the league, really) that those are the most efficient shots in terms of their point value and probability of going in, and he's smart enough to understand that.

Remember I said that no game would ever be decided by a geometry test? It turns out that's not quite true. It was Giannis's understanding of numbers, his willingness to see the game as more than just a physical game, that has allowed him and countless other athletes and GMs to transform basketball over the last few years. It was their hunger to win that made them explore every possible avenue for improvements.

Your hunger can lead you down a similar path. If you're in school right now, coasting through easy classes might not be good for your game.

You'd be amazed at what they talk about around conference rooms inside practice facilities, where you think it's just people pumping iron and sitting in ice baths. Think about how Harden and the Houston Rockets' front office talk about analytics. Last season, they set themselves the goal of scoring 1.16 points per possession, which would make them the most efficient offense in NBA history. To see if they were on track to meet that goal, they had to figure out where on the floor their shots were coming from, which shots increased the probability of drawing a foul, and which shots were actually a waste of a possession. In the old NBA, if you were open for a midrange jumper, you took it. In today's analytically minded sport, that's the worst shot you can take—because the probability of connecting isn't much better than the probability on a three-point shot, except the shot is worth a point less. Multiply that difference over the course of a game, and over the course of a season, and it turns into the difference between a playoff team and a lottery team. That's the kind of math that's going on in nearly every practice facility right now. And if you can't keep up with it, the coach will find someone else who can.

Think about that. For decades, basketball was essentially the same game—see open shot, take open shot—until some of the brightest minds in the game figured out that it wasn't that simple. They revolutionized the game by *thinking* about it more creatively. That was the insight that gave us Damian Lillard and Steph and Kevin Durant. That came from somebody *studying* the game, not playing it with brute force.

My career ended a bit before the analytic revolution really took off, but I still took it to heart that basketball is a game you play with your head, not just your legs. Part of the reason is that I've always loved to read and learn about things that weren't directly connected to the game. But a big part of it was the influence of some of my teammates.

I think of Shane Battier in particular. I can't think of another player who took mental preparation as seriously as Shane, and I tried to emulate him. It wasn't just about tracking his own stats through the season. It was about studying the other team's tendencies on offense and defense so we'd be ready to counter them. Gaming out all the scenarios that could take place over the course of 48 minutes, imagining emergency situations and how we'd respond. Stuff like, "OK, if the Spurs are inbounding the ball down three, with a two-for-one possession situation in the last

30 seconds, here are plays they're most likely to run off the inbound, and here's how we defend it." Or, "If we have our smallball lineups in, that gives me a quickness advantage over their center, which means I'm going to be able to pop out for some corner threes." Shane ate that kind of stuff up, and I loved watching him think.

And it goes beyond strategy. You have to envision yourself playing the game before you play it. You have to really visualize getting back on D after a missed shot. You have to imagine the crowd noise and the trash talk before you hear it. You have to envision all of the different ways your body is going to be hurting by the fourth quarter.

And when you actually live through those things, you find that your surprises are minimized. In a way, you've already lived through it all before. Mental toughness isn't something you just "have" or not. It's something you build up like any other muscle— by envisioning all of your worst-case scenarios, in a calm state of mind, and gaming out your response. It's not just toughness you're building up—it's trust. Trust in your skill, your preparation, your jumper. Trust in your preparation—so that when the other team makes a run, you know that you'll be ready to counter. Trust in your teammates. You have to condition your mind so thoroughly that when the game is on the line, you don't even think about whether or not you trust the guy next to you. You just do.

People like Shane Battier have always inspired me to keep

pushing myself—not just to study the game more, but to expand my mind in general. One off-season, I taught myself to code. Another, I took guitar lessons. Even my exploration into fashion was part of widening my creative understanding of the world. I've always thought of myself as more than a basketball player, even when I was playing the sport. But the trick is that thinking of myself as more than a basketball player actually helped me to be better at basketball. It gave me something to take out my frustrations on, it gave me stuff to talk to my teammates about, it gave me hobbies to keep me out of trouble. During the playoffs, I would cook dinner in the evenings. It helped me get my mind off the situations in the media or on the court. It helped me focus on the task at hand.

Growing up, when you watch your heroes on TV, it looks like they never have doubts or self-criticism—because you just see them from the outside. But when you try to follow in their footsteps, you realize there's no way to succeed in this without facing down your doubts. I'm not proud to admit it, but back in high school or middle school, when I'd have a bad game, sometimes I'd just break down afterward. I'd let the trash talk get to me. I'd lose sleep. Teammates would come up to me the next day and ask if I was OK.

But over the years, I built up my mental toughness. My interests off the court weren't a distraction from that—they were how I made myself tougher. When I started to doubt myself on the court—*What if I let my teammates down when they need me? What if I embarrass myself in front of the fans?*—having a life outside the game reminded me of how much bigger the world is. It helped me overcome those worries by putting them in perspective.

Of course, it wasn't perfect. Over the years, I trained myself not to get baited by trash talk, to keep my head down and let my game do the talking. Well, one night when I was still on the Raptors, we were playing the Celtics—this was the year they formed their "Big Three," and they were feeling themselves. I was on Kevin Garnett most of the night, and KG is a guy who loves to get himself fired up by talking trash. And for some reason, I let him suck me into it. We were jawing at each other all the way up and down the court for the whole night. KG was a player who thrived on that, and I wasn't—so I was giving him a huge mental advantage. And, not coincidentally, I got dominated.

Fortunately, a night like that was more the exception than the rule. But the reason it was an exception was because I practiced mental toughness just like I practiced my jumper.

As I said, visualizing the game before it unfolds is a huge part of that. But sometimes the biggest reserves of mental toughness come from way outside the game—whatever your game is. Winston Churchill is probably up there with the most mentally tough people who ever lived. And when he wasn't fighting Nazis, he was painting. He even wrote a book about it. I don't think he loved painting because he was into some vague ideal of being "well-rounded." It was because, in real life-or-death situations, he needed the perspective and calm that comes with taking a big step back.

You can tell I'm partial to out-of-the-box learning. Yeah, I think it's cool that Damian Lillard has put out some rap albums, but I think it's also cool that NFL offensive lineman John Urschel began a math PhD program at MIT while he was still playing, and that nose tackle Steve McLendon has been taking ballet since he was in college. He said that ballet is "harder than anything else I do"—and this from a guy who lines up across from 325-pound offensive linemen every week. But ballet also gave him the flexibility and body control to excel at his day job. And he's not the only one: Running back Herschel Walker was doing ballet all the way back in the 1980s. Evander Holyfield used ballet workouts to stay fit for the boxing ring, and NHL goalie Ray Emery credited ballet with helping him come back from a serious hip injury. And it's not just athletes, either. Mae Jemison, the first black woman in space, also studied and practiced dance.

In fact, I think some of the most successful athletes get the most value from exposure to ideas outside their field of expertise. The book Candace Parker credits for her mental toughness is *Chop Wood, Carry Water*. Tom Brady likes *The Inner Game of Tennis*, which obviously isn't about football at all. I've gotten real athletic benefits from books about ancient philosophy, martial arts, science, psychology, and so many other topics.

So I am convinced that cultivating your mind will make you a better athlete—or, more generally, that it will help you excel at a high level in whatever you pursue. But beyond that, it will make you *more* than an athlete. When I think about how Carmelo Anthony has become a leader on social issues off the court, and about how he's preparing to excel in his life after basketball, I think about all the work he's had to put in on things that aren't his jumper or his 40 time.

Cultivating your mind matters for that period in your life—and it's a short one in the scheme of things—when you're trying to excel at your sport. But like I said, if you're lucky, there's going to be an afterward. A long one. And what matters most is whether you've stocked your mind with enough learning, interests, and passions—and, just as importantly, the ability to develop new passions—to keep yourself company for the decades of your life that come after you've laced it up the last time. The difference between athletes who have rich, rewarding lives after they hang up their sneakers and athletes whose post-sports lives are one big letdown lies mainly in how hard they've worked at cultivating their minds.

No matter how high you climb in your sport, you don't want to be an old athlete with nothing to think about or talk about but memories of the glory days. You want to keep learning and growing until the day you die. And so you have to start now.

# LETTER 5

# COMMUNICATION IS KEY

R ed. Center. Nail. Zone. Block. Key. Weak. Strong. Bottom. Down.

Out of context, those words probably don't mean much to most people. But if you live and breathe basketball, it's a second language, maybe even closer to something like your native tongue. A few of those words, said at the right time, can open up a whole world of meaning, unlocking whole schemes and action plans that have been practiced thousands of times. Even a hand sign for one of them, tossed up by an exhausted player to a teammate at a critical comment, can save the game or an entire season.

Of course, every game has a language of its own. For football, it's nickel or 4–3 or hot read or "check with me." On the soccer pitch, it's box or dummy run or near post. Chess players say *en passant* or castling. Water polo players might talk about a dry pass or an eggbeater. Curlers have biters, burned stones, shot rock, and the button. A catcher flashes a few fingers, then a few different ones if there's a runner on second. A player mutters something into a jersey so the TV cameras can't see. A coach shouts *Pull! Pull!* to the breaststroker as they pop up for air.

Each team might have their own language, which, taken on its own, can sound like gibberish. Athletes can use phrases that might make sense in one context and yet be totally unfamiliar in another: You know what a button is when you're getting dressed in the morning, but what is it when a guy with a broom is yelling about it on a curling rink? A big part of learning to play a game at a high level is actually learning the language.

There's a reason for that: When every second counts, when 250-pound competitors who want to win as bad as you are flying at you at full speed, and you need to get your teammates on the same page, you need to convey the maximum amount of information in the minimum amount of time. With a few well-chosen words, a skilled player can let everyone on his or her team know what play is about to happen, who should be where, what defensive coverage they're going to be facing, and what to expect next. They can warn them about repeated mistakes, they can center them amid the chaos and the noise of play. If you listen to a great point guard, like Chris Paul or Luka Dončić, they sound like air traffic controllers out there, coordinating a bunch of fast-moving objects as efficiently as possible, with no words to waste. They are also acting like therapists, calming and reassuring, guiding and inspiring.

When the game is on, when you're bone-ass tired, when the crowd is roaring like it's the Roman Colosseum, and it feels like your life is on the line, communication becomes—well, a lifeline. It's what makes five individual athletes into a *team*—a group of guys who have each other's back at the toughest moments.

Imagine things happening so fast that you can't keep up. You're guarding Anthony Davis, who's screening for Danny Green, and at the same time Dwight Howard is setting a back screen for LeBron James.

SCREEN RIGHT! SCREEN RIGHT! WATCH THE SCREEN!

Those words are telling you that you're a split second away from colliding with a wall of muscle at full speed, and you'd better plan accordingly.

If your teammate saw it and told you in time, he was saving you a lot of pain, and maybe saving the play for your defense. If he neglected to tell you—well, if you were pissed with him on the sideline at the next timeout, I wouldn't blame you.

But let's say he warned you in time, and you fought through the screen. Now there are 14 seconds left on the clock. After the initial action, AD sprints to the top of the key to set a high screen for Rajon Rondo. Rondo's either shooting coming off the screen, or AD's rolling into the paint for the pass and the easy bucket. If you want to stop that outcome, you can switch, so that the guy guarding Rondo is now on AD. But wait—the guy on Rondo is probably a lot smaller than AD, which means that AD has a mismatch he can exploit down low, unless one of your other big guys rotates over to help on D.

All of that thinking, all of that anticipation and reaction, has to happen in the span of a few seconds, while you're running at full tilt. Now, some of it is just automatic—that's the point of practice. But *some* of it has to be figured out and communicated in real time. Because no matter how smart you are, and no matter how good your court vision is, there is more happening on the court at any one time than any one person can take in. You need to be able to process the situation with five pairs of eyes, or you're getting steamrolled. And you have to communicate it in a way that's quick, unmistakable, and—just as important—comprehensible over the noise of twenty thousand screaming fans. It's not enough to remember your responsibilities on the court. You have to be part of an organism that can adjust to change in real time. That's communication.

Now do it 200 more times. Because nearly every NBA team averages at least 100 possessions per game, which means that you have to run through something like the situation I described 100 times on offense and 100 times on defense, plus inbounds plays coming out of timeouts, fast breaks off missed free throws, and then whatever adjustments your coaches want to make at halftime while they yell at you for all the times you didn't get it right during the 100-plus possessions in the first half. The teams that communicate efficiently and effectively thrive under those conditions. The teams that don't get caught looking dumb, staring at each other in confusion as the jumbotron shows the replay of their defensive breakdown and the scoreboard adds to the tally of points they keep giving away.

You probably know what the results look like, even if you can't pinpoint *why* they happened. "How did they leave the best shooter on the court wide open from the corner?" "How did a center end up with an uncontested dunk?" "How did that guy get laid out by a pick he didn't see coming—*at the logo*?"

Nine times out of ten, lack of communication.

I've just been talking about one possession in one game, but the lesson holds for every possession—and, really, it goes for life off the court, too.

Because life and leadership are about communication. Communication is the most essential when the stakes are highest.

Here's another scenario from history: Hitler overruns Europe, and Winston Churchill comes to power in Britain. Yes, he has a plan. Yes, he has the world's greatest navy in his pocket. Yes, he has the might of the British Empire behind him and soon enough America, too. But that wouldn't have meant very much without communication. In fact, he probably couldn't have pulled America into the war without his speeches. Without his brilliance on the radio and in the House of Commons. Without those beautiful, haunting words that inspired and coaxed greatness and courage from an empire that was struggling and gasping for air:

The whole fury and might of the enemy must very soon be turned on us. Hitler knows that he will have to break us in this island or lose the war. If we can stand up to him, all Europe may be freed and the life of the world may move forward into broad, sunlit uplands.

But if we fail, then the whole world, including the United States, including all that we have known and cared for, will sink into the abyss of a new dark age made more sinister, and perhaps more protracted, by the lights of perverted science.

Let us therefore brace ourselves to our duties, and so bear ourselves, that if the British Empire and its Commonwealth last for a thousand years, men will still say, "This was their finest hour."

If that doesn't make you want to run through a brick wall . . . then no words will ever work on you. Because that is about the finest bit of communication from a leader ever put together in the English language.

I don't mean to compare basketball to fighting the Nazis. Of course, one is just a game, and the other was a life-and-death struggle. But look, there's a reason the original Olympic sports— things like throwing a javelin, sprinting, and wrestling—were modeled closely on the activities a soldier had to excel at. There's a reason why, in the epic of the *Iliad*, when the Greek heroes get a break from fighting the war, an athletic competition breaks out. It's also why no battle was ever fought, just like no big game was ever played, without an inspiring message spoken to the troops.

"One must speak to the soul," Napoleon said of the speeches he made to his men before they charged the enemy. "It is the only way to electrify the men."

Sports and war have long been held to have important things in common: They mean struggling against an opponent, against chaos, against fatigue, and against ego. They require us to risk our physical well-being, in more or less serious ways. Success in either requires a combination of individual excellence and total commitment to a team.

And in either realm, there needs to be the person who says exactly the right words at exactly the right moment. It can be as straightforward as "SCREEN RIGHT!" or as eloquent as "This was their finest hour." It can be a quiet nod or a reassuring hand after a missed free throw.

In whatever form, a leader sees the challenge ahead, knows what the members of the team need to do to meet the challenge, and knows the words or the symbols or the images that will get them where they need to be. Knowing *that* doesn't just take charisma: It takes a huge amount of insight into the team members. What kinds of words motivate them, and what kinds of words turn them off? How far can they be pushed? Is this a time to pick up their spirits, or a time to get them to ratchet up the intensity? Leaders have to know all that before they find the right words.

Now, I know that plenty of coaches and athletes take this sports/war analogy too far. Some coaches use it as an excuse to be abusive to their players—they're General Patton in their own minds, and cursing out a guy for missing a free throw is just the cost of victory. Some players use it as an excuse from the obligation to be a decent person. It's the truth, so why not tweet it, right? If you're a warrior, you get to be an asshole, right? But for the most part—though, sure, there are exceptions—the most effective coaches and the most talented players are the opposite of assholes. They're secure enough that they let their success speak for itself—and when they communicate, they're trying to build you up, not to dominate you.

So I'm not saying you need to take this analogy and run with it. I'm just saying that in high-intensity situations, the difference between effective and ineffective communication is instantly apparent, because the difference truly matters. When the stakes are low—when you're trying to sound smart in a pointless office meeting, for instance—that's when the BS comes out, stuff like, "We need to circle back and do a deep dive on optimizing our synergies." Everyone knows that doesn't mean anything, but because the stakes are low, it doesn't matter. When the stakes are high—when winning or losing comes down to knowing those other four guys on the floor have your back—communication needs to be sharp, direct, and to the point.

Communicating effectively on the court is something I always took pride in—even though it took some work. Some guys are just naturally vocal on the court. I'm not, so I had to practice communication just like I had to work on my shot or my conditioning.

But that's why I was so proud of becoming a better communicator over the course of my career. In particular, I loved communicating on D. With the Heat, since I had to sacrifice a little on the offensive end, I wanted to make sure I was standing out on the other end. I felt like it was my responsibility to make sure the defense was always solid, and I could do that by keeping up a running stream of communication with my teammates, letting them know where I was at all times, and where the attacking players were in relation to them. And then, of course, I backed up my words with actions—I wanted my teammates to trust that I was going to be where I said I'd be. I think this constant talking on D really helped us as a team. Talking while playing defense became a habit. In fact, as a coach once told me, "If you're not talking, you're not playing defense."

Man, even that is a great example of great communication: *If you're not talking, you're not playing defense.*

I remembered that line every single game for the rest of my career. I hope you do, too.

On all of the teams I've been on, I found that the more I communicated, the more my teammates communicated. It becomes part of your team identity—it's infectious. And when the communication is clicking, it's a great feeling. Communicating became one of my favorite facets of the game. You don't even have to have the most talent to be a great communicator—you just have to be loud.

Like every habit, it can feel a bit weird at first. *I'm already running at a full sprint, now I have to use some of my oxygen to yell at my teammates who should already know what they need to do while I'm doing it, too?* It can even feel a bit silly, like you're narrating what you're doing while you're doing it. But do it enough, and you'll get over it. Remember, each player on the court has access to some information that the other players don't. So when you share that information, it's like you're becoming exponentially smarter as a unit. And you'll see it pay off—in crisp rotations, in more defensive stops, in preventing bad shots with the shot clock winding down, in forced turnovers. Success is a great way to get over the feeling that barking at your teammates is weird. There are few better feelings on defense than having a teammate shout out a screen, then going over the top of it to beat your man to his spot and deny him the shot that screen was meant to pop free.

But it doesn't stop there. Knowing how to communicate is key to keeping your team on the same page throughout the season, especially after losses. It's easier to keep communication open when things are going well. You probably know the saying: "Everyone gets along on a winning team." It's harder—but much more important—to keep communication open when things *aren't* going well.

After a disappointing loss, the most important thing to do is to break down what went wrong—honestly, but also respectfully.

Communication is even more important when you've had a setback. The more you're underperforming your expectations, the more you need to talk—that's the only reliable way to turn things around.

You might think that good athletes are so intense that when they lose, they immediately start tearing into each other and arguing in the locker room, coaches ripping into players, and players trying to deflect the blame onto their teammates. But good teams, in my experience, don't really do that—losing teams do. Losing teams also shut down and stop talking when things go bad. They close off. They stop helping each other. They don't talk. They just stew.

It's hard to say what's cause and what's effect, but I think it goes both ways. Bad teams take their frustration out on one another. But doing that also makes them worse, because they can't honestly assess what they need to do to get better. When everyone is afraid of a fight breaking out, no one is honest. When people are closed off, no one is connected. And when everyone is angry, talking after a game becomes all about dragging others down, rather than about listening to the criticism you need to improve. It's close to a rule: The better the communication, the better the team.

These days, I feel like communication is something of a lost art. Maybe it's just because I'm a retired player, and retired players love to talk about how much better things were back in the day—all you need to do is watch Chuck on the *NBA on TNT* postgame show to know that—but I swear I see teams communicating less on defense these days. That's a big mistake. Not only is every team that misses a chance to communicate also missing out on an advantage it can take over the other team; it's also putting itself at a disadvantage against teams that feature some of the most elite athletes the world has ever seen. Giannis, Steph and Klay, Harden and Westbrook, LeBron and AD, KD and Kyrie Irving. Those dudes will beat you consistently on your best day. If you're not communicating, they will beat you like you stole something.

With the Heat, that was an advantage we were always searching for. Before a playoff series, we'd go in depth and talk about our game plan, what we wanted to do, and how we were going to do it. We'd walk through plays and game out the opponent's response. We'd think about how specific plays would work, or might break down, in specific game scenarios. And when you're communicating with pros who have been there before, it's not as if the coach is directing everything, like a teacher in a classroom. The coach is talking to us about what he expects, and we're talking to each other. I might talk to Shane about rotating on defense. Shane might talk to Mario Chalmers about the pick-and-roll. And Mario might remind Dwyane Wade how he's going to guard Tony Parker. The more talking, the better.

If you saw those Heat teams on the court, you probably always saw us jawing back and forth with Mario. But that was all part of it, for us. On the outside, it may have looked like we were arguing. But we knew exactly what we were doing. We were all competitors. We all wanted to win. And Rio was one of the most passionate guys on the team—that's what you were seeing when we were going back and forth after a play. He'd correct me if he thought I did something wrong, I'd get back at him, and we'd debate it. There's nothing wrong with a debate. But there's a big difference between that and the kind of reckless yelling you see in a losing, undisciplined team. The difference is that Rio and I, and all of our teammates, really did care about building each other up, because that was the only way we were going to be able to play championship basketball. We would debate, fix the issue, and move on.

Coach Spoelstra was part of that, too. Like I said, I remember being uncomfortable with my role in the offense, and Spo took it upon himself to make me feel comfortable. It took a lot of hard conversations—on the court, at dinner, in his office—but he modeled so much patience that I took it to heart. And he created the kind of team atmosphere where I didn't have to shove that discomfort down and pretend everything was fine. He helped to build the kind of environment where I felt like I could speak my truth, rather than one where I had to keep it bottled up until the stress got to be too much. Instead of just yelling, "Hey, give me the damn ball," like I felt tempted to do at times, instead of letting my frustration fester and boil over, I talked it out with Coach, and got to a place where I felt like I was contributing everything I could to make the team a champion.

As I became a more mature player, I found that more and more of the responsibility of communication was falling on me. That's the way it's supposed to be—that's what teams expect from their veteran players. But leading as a veteran isn't about chewing guys out when a play goes wrong. It's about knowing each one of your teammates, and understanding how to motivate them. Some guys get fired up when you yell at them. Other guys say, "Hey, I don't like yelling. It just throws me off my game." You have to know the difference. A good communicator knows how to discover and respond to those differences. A good communicator knows that each teammate and each situation is unique—what works with one guy in a certain game scenario will backfire with another guy in a different scenario. We talked earlier about the importance of cultivating your mind. Part of that is learning to be a better psychologist—someone who understands your teammates' quirks, but also someone who has observed enough people that you can start picking out patterns. With enough practice, you can tell the difference between the kind of teammate who needs a direct challenge and the kind of teammate who needs a quiet word. With great leaders, it can look intuitive, but it's really the result of a lot of study and observation.

You have to spend time with your teammates off the court—at dinner, at each other's houses, wherever. It can't be all business all the time, because you have to build up trust and comfort with one another so that when you *do* have to call them out, they know it's coming from a place of respect. They know it's coming from the heart. That way, problems don't boil over. They realize, "This guy's a person just like me. He struggles to get better, too, so I know where he's coming from."

Part of communicating at a high level is learning to take your ego out of it, and learning not to attack other people's egos. You're not criticizing a teammate to make him or her feel bad, or to make yourself feel better—you're doing it to solve a particular problem. You're going to solve that problem a lot more effectively if the target of your criticism comes away feeling better rather than worse. One of the great military and political leaders of the twentieth century, Dwight Eisenhower, said that he never dealt in "personalities." What he meant was that he criticized issues and actions, not people. It's the simple difference between "I need reports on my desk on time" and "You're too lazy to get your reports in on time." Or worse, what you see in sports, where a coach or a player specifically calls out other players in front of the team to shame or embarrass them.

Communication should help you get the best out of people. It should not be about making them feel *worse*.

And you've got to be able to take it, too. That's the part of communication that many would-be leaders miss. You can't just dish, dish, dish, and then storm off in a huff when someone tries to fix something about your game. People know it instinctively— no one respects a guy who dishes it out but can't take it. Remember, when you're responding to criticism, you're modeling the way others are going to respond to you. If you lash out at others, you're increasing the chances they'll lash out at you. If you listen patiently and take criticism in stride, you're increasing the chances that you're going to get listened to down the road. Communication has to go both ways, or it doesn't work. And we've talked about this before—if you're really hungry to improve your craft, you'll welcome all the criticism you get, because every critique is a chance to get better at some aspect of the game.

When things blow up—when teams get into that destructive spiral of losing, and anger, and suspicion, and ego—it's often because the lines of communication broke down. Innocent comments get interpreted in the worst possible light. Misunderstandings proliferate. Everyone starts seeing the worst in each other. It's like going through a breakup, except with ten or twenty other people, and you're stuck together until the end of the season.

That's when having steady veteran leaders can matter the most. You need people to mediate—to say, "No, no, no, that's not what he meant. What did you hear when he said X? What did you mean when you said Y?" It takes a lot of patience and a lot of tolerance. But it pays off.

The point is that really strong leaders know how to have hard conversations without upsetting the team dynamic. They know how to take criticism like an adult, and they know how to give criticism in a way that leads to results. They've learned that communicating with teammates and coaches isn't about figuring out who to pin the blame on when things go wrong. It's about identifying problems and getting to the root of them—about helping people understand what's happening.

And getting better at it is a lifelong effort. My good friend Juwan Howard is now the head coach at Michigan. When we were teammates, we always talked about how important communication was to success on and off the court. Now he's in a new situation, trying to teach and inspire a group of players who are young enough to be his kids. He told me that his communication techniques are constantly evolving. When we were in the NBA together, group texts weren't really a thing. Now they're his go-to way for starting a conversation with his players.

It would be easy for Juwan to stop putting in the work and to stick with whatever worked for him when he was at Michigan back in the early '90s with the Fab Five. He could just say something like, "Kids these days, they're too me-first to be coached." You can always find an excuse for staying in your shell, whether it's generational differences, or differences in background or upbringing, or differences in skill level. But you'd be surprised what happens when you get over those excuses. I've seen the unlikeliest of friendships develop on teams because two people found a common ground they didn't know they had. Juwan knows that, too, and that's what has made him successful as a coach.

It's the same quality that makes Coach K one of the greatest of all time. I mentioned my experience on the Olympic team with Coach K a few letters ago. And it's a great reminder that communicating on a successful team isn't just about reaming people out when they fail—it's about letting people know that you see their strengths, making them feel confident in their own game. Even NBA players—even Olympic athletes—need that kind of encouragement from time to time.

So when Coach K told me he was impressed by my wingspan on defense, that's the first time I thought, "Wow, you know what? I think I know how I'm going to play on this team. I know my value with this team. I'm going to excel on defense." If I hadn't heard that, I probably would have gotten the wrong idea about how I could contribute on the team. I probably would've gotten lost in the shuffle. Hell, we've got LeBron, Kobe, Wade, Carmelo—not many shots left after that.

But there's a reason Coach K is so good at what he does. He's a great communicator. He knew how I could contribute, and he knew how to put the idea in my head. If it had been something like, "Chris, we just don't need you on offense," it would have hurt my pride, and I probably would have tuned out. Coach K knew that, so instead he told me what I needed to hear in a way that made it more likely that I would actually hear it.

And beyond that, I'll give myself some credit for listening, too—for getting that Coach K wasn't just saying something about my defense to be nice, but because he was sending a message about where I needed to put in the most effort. Listening is the other side of communication. It's about actually taking time to think about what you're being told, about taking enough time to be quiet that you can actually hear what others have to say. Listening is the underrated half of communication—there are tons of books about "Great Speeches of History" and probably not any about "Great Listeners of History"—but it's a skill you can develop like any other.

It's been fascinating to observe how the loudest talkers on any team probably aren't the best listeners—but that the real leaders know how to do both. When it's time for them to talk, they get right to the point. When you're talking to them, they make you feel like you have 100 percent of their attention.

I haven't communicated on a basketball court the way I used to since 2016. These days I communicate in other ways: As a father. As a TV analyst. As a writer. As an activist. What I'm talking about these days has changed—but the lessons in communication I've learned over my athletic career have been enduring ones. Know your audience. Be honest and to the point. If you want to earn the right to be heard, remember to listen. Nothing I learned on the court has served me as well, or in as many different contexts, as what I learned about communication. Basketball has its own language—but the truths of good communication are universal.

It's the same with you. Whatever path your career takes, your playing days are going to come to an end eventually. And when they do, what you learned about how to talk and how to listen will be one of the most valuable things you take with you.

The words may change—but the task itself never does.

# LETTER 6

## SWEEP AWAY YOUR EGO

'm not saying you're an egomaniac. But I'm saying you've got an ego.

I'm saying it's a problem. It's a problem for everyone.

Ego is that voice whispering in your ear.

Ego is that impulse to beat your chest and say, "I have nothing to learn from you"—from anyone.

Ego keeps you from passing the ball to a teammate because *you* want to be The Guy, not him.

Ego makes you think you know more than Coach.

Ego is the tempting voice that says, "I don't need to show respect or kindness. I'm gonna go pro and get rich."

Ego is what makes people say stuff like, "Do you even know who I am?"

Ego is the kid who quits the team because "Coach is out to get me."

Ego is thinking that everyone you meet is a supporting player in the Story of You.

Ego is one of those things that's hard to define exactly. But you know it when you see it.

And it's never something good to see in your coaches, your teammates, or your friends. It's what makes coaches yell at kids for no reason. It's what turns promising young players into ball hogs. It's what makes people—on the court and off—act like jerks.

And what's especially dangerous about ego is that, as easy as it is to see in other people, it's really hard to see in the mirror. Ego could be distorting your life, your relationships, your game right now—and unless you're really good at introspection, you'd have no idea.

It's obvious *how* ego holds people back, but we have trouble seeing *where* it's holding us back.

That's why I am writing this warning to you: You must be ruthless about keeping your ego in check. You must attack the enemy within, because ego is indeed the enemy of all the things you want to accomplish in the game and in life.

I remember there was a guy I played against as a kid. He was blessed with speed, height, and a smooth jumper. He got drafted straight out of high school, while the rest of us in that class spent at least a year or two in college. But then the team he was drafted by wanted to have him play in what's now called the G-League for a season.

He wasn't having it. No way, he told a reporter. I'm good enough for the NBA *right now*. I am *not* a developmental player, he said. That's ego, man. If you think you're as good as you can be, you're right. You won't get any better. If you think there is something shameful about being coached or worked with, you're never advancing to that next level.

The team cut him after two seasons. It was cautionary tale for me, and I hope it's one for you.

The G-League used to be called the D-League, and guys took that wrong. I think they thought "D" stood for Deficient—like a D grade in school. Nah. D was short for *developmental*. Guys like J. J. Barea, Danny Green, and Hassan Whiteside all came out of the D-League.

Who doesn't want to develop? What was the slur in that? Why are some young players so averse to that?

Ego is a big part.

Managing ego is one of the hardest things in the world, especially when you're young. Especially when you're talented. Every human being is susceptible to ego, but let me tell you, it's even harder when you're young and other people are telling you how great you are.

Or when people are bending the rules for you. It's hard when your success depends in no small part on your belief in yourself.

It seems like almost every week there is a piece on ESPN

about some generational talent and *what could have been*. It's rarely an injury that took them out of the game. It always something else. Drugs. The law. Thinking they were God's gift to the game. It's so tempting to see yourself as the franchise player, the indispensable one. But that is rarely true. It's way more common for No. 1 draft picks to fail to live up to expectations than it is for them to exceed them.

Why is that? Ego is a big part of it, and nothing fuels ego quite like everyone telling you you're great.

And look, I'm not being harsh on these guys to set myself up as some kind of superior being who's never had an egotistical thought a day in his life. I'm harsh on them because I recognize in their stories the same kind of ego that almost derailed my own career, more than once. Hearing stories about talent going to waste because of ego is so frustrating to me because I hear those stories and think, *That could have easily been me.*

I always wanted to be The Man. I always, always wanted to just be the best. I was like any other kid you see playing basketball in the driveway—it was always Game 7, and I was always hitting the winning shot at the buzzer. (If I missed, the imaginary refs always put more time back on the clock.) If there was anything that separated me from other kids, it's just that I wanted it *so much*. No good athlete becomes *the best* without wanting to be the best, in a way that's almost unhealthy. It's a key skill. It's also a key danger. For as long as there has been sports, there have been young athletes discovering that the skills that made them *the best* at one level just won't cut it at the next one.

It's a story as old as competition itself: An athlete shows promise, so they get a chance to perform on a bigger stage. It's the wrestler from Piraeus being invited to compete at the Olympics in 316 BCE. It's the high school linebacker getting recruited by Nick Saban to play at Alabama. It's the fantastic one-and-done player being drafted to play in the NBA. The gymnast trying to qualify for the Olympics.

What do each of them find? That this new level of competition is *nothing* like what they have ever faced before. Suddenly, they're not only not the best, they're getting their butt kicked. It happened to Kobe. It happened to Jeter. It happened to Brady. It happened to Rapinoe. It happened to basically every great player you've ever heard of. You go from being the best at your old level to the bottom of the heap (or, at best, the middle of the pack) at the new level. How you respond to this sudden change in the level of play defines you. It's what separates the amateurs from the pros—literally.

And how you respond is all about your ego. If you keep telling yourself that you're still the best—even when the facts tell you that you have a lot to learn—you'll end up washing out, and some new young stud will take your place. You'd be surprised how long you can blame your failures on the bigger stage to bad luck, or the coach having it in for you, or your teammates not deferring to your brilliance. But if you're humble enough to look reality in the face—to realize that you still have a huge amount of learning and growing to do—then you really do have a shot at greatness. That's the paradox of ego: If you want to be great, you have to be honest with yourself about all the ways in which you're not great yet.

I learned that from experience. I got recruited by Georgia Tech because I excelled in high school ball. I thought college would be more of the same. I couldn't have been more wrong. College was a kick in the nuts. It just wasn't as fun as I thought it was supposed to be, and the main reason was that I was on the next level, and the success I took for granted in high school wasn't coming as easy. Going from being a high school standout to having to earn my minutes like everyone else seriously hurt my pride, and then when I got on the floor, I was facing guys used to playing against ACC-level competition. I struggled to keep up with the pace; you can bet it hurt my confidence.

That was my first taste of what it meant to struggle on the next level. I wasn't automatically the best anymore—I was just another guy. Paul Hewitt, our coach, was really good at breaking us down and building us back up again. And that meant getting my ass handed to me by the older guys on the team, three-hour practice after three-hour practice, and then weights, and then individual workouts, and then class. It was just grueling.

But it made a difference. I stuck with the program, I learned from Coach Hewitt, and eventually I got drafted into the pros. And that meant another "next level"—doing the same thing all over again, this time getting thrown into practice and games as an NBA rookie against guys who had been in the league for years. I'm not complaining—I'm just pointing out that the experience of making it to the next level isn't what it looks like on TV. And I'm letting you know that the main thing that got me over the hump both times wasn't my height or my speed or any other physical gifts—it was the ability to keep my ego in check, to get my ass kicked in practice and say, "Damn. I have a long way to go." Being able to tell yourself that is the difference between making it to the next level—whether it's in sports, or in academics, or in your career—and stalling out.

But it was a struggle every step of the way. I'd never played against guys so strong—and this was an era in which the game was a lot more physical, and in which big guys like me had to play down low a lot more than they do now. Just like it was when I started at Georgia Tech, I couldn't expect to dominate. And just as the mentality of college was different from the mentality of high school, being in the pros was different again. In college, your teammates are your dorm-mates. When you're not practicing together, you're chilling together. But now on the Raptors, it was all business. I was the kid on a team full of grown men who had their own lives and weren't expecting to hang out after practice. And as a young kid, that's hard to adjust to, not to mention living in another country with cold winters.

Despite that, I still had my ego to contend with. All of my mental energy was focused on scoring, on getting the most points on the stat sheet. If I wasn't getting my points, I'd go into a funk, and my effort on defense went to hell.

Sam Mitchell, one of our coaches on the Raptors, noticed the pattern. And after one game, he took me aside and said, "It's unacceptable to be the best player on the court with the ball in your hands, and not also be the best with the ball *not* in your hands." He even benched me one night in San Antonio on the road. I got the message. If I wanted to be the focus of our team's offense on one end, I had to prove it on the other end. Some nights, your shot just isn't falling. But you can give 100 percent effort on defense *every* night—that was up to me. That was always under my control.

I let that sink in, and it changed my approach to the game. I learned to keep my head up when my shots weren't falling, and I learned that I had to be a leader at both ends if I wanted my teammates to take me seriously. But ego is powerful. My ego was still there, barking at me that I was better than my stats said, that I deserved more minutes, more respect, more media attention. At times, it really cost me and my teammates.

In 2006, I was on the U.S. World Championship Team. It was the year we lost to Greece in the semifinals. It was not a proud moment in American sports history. But looking back, it wasn't a proud moment in my life either. I was fully in the sway of my own ego. I mean, I wasn't like full-blown Kanye West with my ego, but it was holding me back.

All I was thinking about during that tournament was my own

playing time. I was so pissed that I wasn't getting my due. Over the course of the tournament, I played fewer than 14 minutes a game. For someone used to playing a starter's minutes, and getting a starter's stats, that stung. I wasn't used to coming off the bench to contribute.

It should have been a highlight of my career, starter's minutes or not. I was representing my country. I was playing alongside the best in the game. I could have learned a lot from them, if I had gotten my head out of my ass. At the very least, I could have enjoyed the free trip to Japan for the tournament, right? But instead, it was days of feeling sorry for myself. It was days fuming at my coaches for not appreciating me enough. Mostly it was just me, me, me. I wasn't thinking about the team. I wasn't thinking of contributing, of cheering for my teammates from the bench, or of playing my ass off in the minutes I did get. I wasn't thinking of anything much but what I wanted. That's what ego does.

Now, I never had a blowup with the coaches or my teammates. I kept my head down and said the right things in public. But humans are really, really good at reading each other's hidden feelings—we're social animals, and that's what we've evolved to do. Anyone within five feet of me would have known instantly that I was pissed, that I wasn't buying in, that I didn't give a damn about the team's success if I couldn't get my minutes. And attitudes like that are contagious.

Did my lack of buy-in hurt the team? Did it contribute to our failure? It's impossible to say—but I can tell you that it didn't help. I was part of the problem.

When I look back on my career, that's a period I really regret. Maybe you can remember moments like that in your life. Where you were a little petulant or selfish, where you were taking value away from your team rather than adding it, where you were refusing to learn and improve because you were just feeling stubborn. Maybe you remember days where the best thing you could have done for your teammates was stay away.

I had to sit with the disappointment of 2006 for a long time, and I came to realize how my self-centeredness hurt the team, even if they didn't know it, and, on an even more basic level, kept me from enjoying my chance to play on the world stage. But that's the thing about fighting your ego: The most powerful step to defeating it is learning to see it in the mirror. Once you realize the role ego plays in holding you back, you've taken a huge step toward beating it.

In 2008, I had my second chance: I was back on the national team for the Olympics, and this time my attitude was, "Whatever it takes to play. Whatever the team needs." I told this story briefly in the last letter, on communication, but I think it's worth unpacking here. It was one evening after training camp in Vegas. Coach K, our head coach, had had some wine at dinner; afterward he came up to me, and what he said specifically was, "Hey, we were watching film, and I saw you on a pick-and-roll. And you had huge arms—they were so long!"

Coach K didn't ask me to do anything, but what I heard was, "This is an opportunity. This is your chance to contribute." He didn't say, "You can be the star of this team." He didn't say, "I see you with the ball with the clock winding down." No, he was talking about something humbler, and what I heard was that he was thinking about the role I'd play with the team, and if I worked to impress him in practice, I'd have a better shot at being a contributor. A couple of years earlier, I would have just heard the compliment and nothing else. Or I would have dismissed the compliment as not "appreciating" what I was capable of doing with the ball in my hands moving toward the basket. I wouldn't have thought about what I needed to do to earn more minutes, because I would have just felt entitled to them. I wouldn't have seen the crack in the door. And been humble enough to stick my foot in there.

And it made a difference. Dwight Howard was our starter, but I was the first one off the bench to replace him in our rotation. I led the team in rebounds. And we brought home the gold medal.

Now, acting as if we lost in 2006 because I was blinded by ego, or as if we won in 2008 because I learned how to contribute off the bench, would just be another way of making this story all about me, instead of about our team. We lost in 2006 and won in 2008 for a ton of reasons that had nothing to do with me. But as far as I'm concerned, the difference is this: In 2006, I was hurting the team, whatever the stats said. In 2008, I was helping, whatever the stats said. No one, not MJ, not Kobe, not LeBron, can win a championship or a gold medal by himself. But every member of a team has the ability to change his contribution from a minus sign to a plus sign. I'm proud of the fact that I was able to do that in 2008.

That's the good news about ego. It's never too late to fix it. If you screw up and hurt your team out of selfishness or frustration? OK, well, the inability to own that, apologize, and grow from the experience? That's ego, too. But looking at your behavior with some awareness, taking responsibility, listening to feedback, and doing better next time? That takes humility. It also takes confidence. So don't dwell. Don't deny. *Improve.*

My proudest moments as a player are the ones where I defeated my ego. In the 2013 Finals against the Spurs, in Game 7, I didn't score a single point. But instead of moping about that, I found ways to contribute on defense and on the boards. I'm proud that we won it all, of course. But I'm also proud of what I'd learned in my years in the game—I'd learned enough to figure out how to put my ego on hold for the sake of the team. Any kid can imagine hitting the winning shot in Game 7. But it takes a real grown-up to figure out how he can still make a difference even when his shot isn't falling. You'd be surprised to hear it, but that made winning Game 7 with zero points on my stat sheet almost sweeter than if I'd put up 20.

When I first came to Miami, I knew what I wanted from our game plan. I wanted the ball on the right block, because that's how I got my points in Toronto. But Coach Spoelstra's system didn't work like that. I had to get out of my comfort zone and accept it—and so did everyone else on that team. We all made sacrifices to make it work, even LeBron and Dwyane.

It's hard to remember looking back on it, but I had no idea whether or not it was going to work. Before I left Toronto, a friend said to me, "Are you really going to leave Toronto to try to win a championship? Hardly anyone wins a championship, man. Stay here. You'll make way more money. We love you in this city." Imagine how hard it was for me to make the decision to leave for Miami, and imagine how hard it was for me to do that while making sure that my ego wasn't driving my decision. I had to work to make sure I was leaving for the right reasons— that they aligned with my why, too—because I really thought I could win, and because I was willing to do whatever it took to win, and because winning was more valuable to me than money. I had to turn down millions of dollars (and the star role I had for the Raptors), but I had to make sure I wasn't doing it out of vanity or greed. It was a bet on myself, a bet that I could do more with D-Wade and LeBron than I could being The Man in Toronto.

Some people say they want to win, but then when someone tells them what they have to do to get the W—to get back on defense on every play, to jump for every single rebound—I've seen people refuse to do it. I've seen it with my own eyes. They don't want to win, they want to *have* won. They only want to do the glamorous parts of winning, not the hard, grinding parts. They'd rather have glory than do the work. The irony is that there's a lot more glory as a grinder on a winning team than as a ball hog on a losing one.

As my teammate Shane Battier put it, "No one asks me what my stats were. They ask to see my rings, and they ask me how I decide which one to wear." That's the irony: Ego tells you that you deserve all the glory, when the most glory you can get comes from being on a winning team. You have to understand: If you play for the name on the front, they'll remember the name on the back.

It takes humility to take that deal. But your ego doesn't get that. Your ego is always going to want more and more. After we won that first championship with the Heat, we added Rashard Lewis and Ray Allen. I knew that I'd be getting a lot fewer shots. But every player on that team recognized their role—and we won our second consecutive title.

The whole time, we had to tune out the voices in our ears telling us that we deserved more—more points, more playing time, more attention.

Do you know how many people are in your ear when you're playing at the highest level? A lot. Think of the people in your ear now and multiply it by millions. And most of those people on the outside looking in are trying to feed your ego. "Why aren't you getting the ball more? You should be getting the ball more. If it was me, I would've . . ." One night, when I was a young player in Toronto, something or other didn't go my way, and I threw a fit—not behind closed doors in the locker room, but right out in public. And that same night, I heard from one of my friends: "It was good that you did that. You gotta stand up for yourself."

People who tell you those sorts of things usually don't mean you harm. Most of that talk comes from friends, people who are just trying to pump you up for the next game. But what they don't realize is that they're just feeding that ego monster, chipping away at the discipline that keeps you from making the team about yourself. It's like a guy trying to hand you a bacon cheeseburger when you're on a diet. If I'd really listened to the friend who cheered me on for throwing a tantrum, I'd have turned into one of those players no one in their right mind wants to play with.

If you get too wrapped up in that kind of talk, the next thing you know, you're taking a bad shot when you should've dished to an open teammate, you're slumped down on the bench because you're having a bad scoring night, you're giving a half-assed effort on defense because of some imaginary slight.

Can you tune all of that out? Can you still play your heart out if you only get ten shots a game? Can you come off the bench, like Steve Kerr asked of Andre Iguodala even though Iggy had been a starter his entire career with the Sixers? Can you run back on defense if the point guard doesn't pass it to you? Can you pick up a teammate when he's down, instead of waiting for someone else to do it? Can you trust that your coaches want to win just as much as you do? Can you learn what you think you already know?

If you can do that, you have the mental strength and the rock-hard humility it takes to succeed at the next level—whatever the next level is.

And when you do succeed, it will grow your confidence—not your ego.

What's the difference between ego and confidence?

Ego is a liar. It tells you you're the greatest, regardless of what the results say—it always finds a way to spin those. Confidence is belief in your ability, in the work you've put in, that's backed up by reality. Confidence is expecting good things to happen because you worked to make them happen.

Ego tells you that you deserve success just because you're you. Confidence tells you that you can reasonably expect to earn success based on how your efforts have paid off in the past.

Ego tells you that you've already achieved all you need to achieve. Confidence is always ready for the next challenge. It's ready to help others, too. Confidence is what I think of when I think of Sue Bird. Bird has four WNBA championships, plus eight All-WNBA selections, eleven All-Star selections, and five Euroleague and Russian championships. She could have retired satisfied with all she accomplished, but she continues to reinvent herself year after year as she gets older, holding a front office job with the NBA's Denver Nuggets then standing up for equal pay and LGBTQ rights with her fiancée, Megan Rapinoe. That's confidence—rightly earned.

Mistaking ego for confidence happens at every level. They make documentaries on that stuff. I've known a lot of basketball players who were talented enough to play in the NBA, but they just got too big-headed. They stopped right there at the finish line. They had one more lap to go in the race, and they started looking at the crowd, and flexing their muscles, and then . . . they didn't even realize they were in last place. Other guys were keeping their heads down, putting in the work, and they lapped them.

I've said it to you before, but I'll say it again to hammer it home: Talent isn't enough. You could make an entire league out of guys with NBA-level talent but not the NBA-level mentality.

Whatever your goal is, you have the power to cultivate that same mentality—the mentality of confidence, not ego—right now. You have to assess your ego every time you make a decision. Stop and think to yourself, "Am I being egotistical right now? Am I putting my own success over team success? What would being a better teammate look like?"

Many years ago, Pat Riley wrote a book called *The Winner Within*. He calls ego "the disease of me." I think that's a great expression. And he talks about how it tears apart winning and losing teams, super-talented and less-talented athletes alike, with equal vigor. Of course, if you meet Pat, you'll see he's as hungry to win as anyone. He wants his teams to know what they can do. But that's the operative word: *they*. Not me, me, me.

Ego poisons success—confidence is necessary for success. Figuring out the difference is the most important realization a young athlete can ever make. And nothing else you do in your time in sports will serve you better as a human being than learning that lesson.

# LETTER 7

## LEADERS LEAD

There is an expression we have for teams without leaders. We call those losing teams.

Because a team without a leader—whether or not there's someone with a captain's C on his jersey—isn't going anywhere.

Like you, I've been hearing about leadership my whole life. Every book by or about athletes is guaranteed to have a section on leadership. Every sports documentary focuses on that critical moment in a game or a season when somebody stepped up and *said what needed to be said*. Every sports movie has that scene, in the locker room, at halftime, in the classroom, where somebody breaks it down and gets through to the person who needed to be shaken out of their stupor.

The truth is that leadership is not so easily pinned down.

When most people who follow sports talk about leadership, they think about the guy the other players can count on to make the key shot—the best player on the team. Or maybe they think about the most vocal player, the one who's always barking at his teammates during timeouts. I know I was just talking to you about the importance of communication, but I don't want that to intimidate you.

Leadership is not just the guy giving speeches.

A leader, to me, is just the person who steps up and does what needs to be done—who becomes what the situation requires. They do that on the court, in the classroom, in their neighbor-hoods, in a crisis, when they see somebody getting bullied, when they see an opportunity in business.

All these situations are different and require different kinds of leadership, but the one thing they have in common is that there is something that needs to be done and somebody who needs to do it.

The question is: Are you that person?

I remember I was sixteen years old when my varsity coach Leonard Bishop asked me to come into his office. It's a meeting a lot of players had with Coach Bishop, that players have had with all coaches in all sports for all time. It's the summoning, the call to leadership. Not all get the call, not all answer it, but I'm telling you, you can't be great without this experience—when someone you respect sees your potential and tells you it's time to step up.

Coach Bishop started telling me about the great players he'd coached over the years and how each one of them had stepped up to lead the team where it needed to go. "We usually think of the leader as the most outspoken athlete, but you know what?" he told me. "You have a different leadership style. You lead by example." And he really opened my eyes to the idea that you don't have to be the loudest to be the leader. He let me know that my teammates were paying attention to me even when I didn't open my mouth.

I was a quiet kid then, and because he was a great leader, Coach Bishop knew me well enough that he had tailored his pitch to me. He told me that I didn't have to lead by giving big inspiring speeches, that I could inspire and guide and lead my teammates in my own unique way: By being on time for practice and class, by trying my best, by being dressed and ready to go for practice, by paying attention. By being an outstanding citizen. By working hard. By showing my commitment. By showing myself as someone who was always learning and always wanting to get better. By taking feedback . . . and giving it. By being someone people looked up to.

People keep their eyes on a leader—how they walk, how they carry themselves—even when it's not game time. That was all leadership—and it was a kind of leadership that fit me especially well. Coach Bishop told me that that was what he was now expecting from me.

It didn't feel like a burden to me. It felt like an honor. I left that room feeling ten feet tall. It's a conversation I think about to this day.

Usually when we think of a leader, it's the person at the front of the charge. It's the coach giving that speech to rile up his team. It's the person with the bullhorn leading the protest. Those things are true—those people are leaders. But maybe because those are the kinds of leadership that *look* most dramatic on a screen, our culture gives us a falsely limited idea of what leadership can be. Even if that's not you, you can still be a leader. Leaders can set the quiet example. They can set the tone for the people around them. Leaders pick their teammates up when things get hard. Leaders support. Leaders don't make the team about them—they make the team better by being a part of it.

I like the saying that you have to learn to follow in order to lead. I truly believe that. If you don't know what it's like to be a good follower, you can never get inside the mind of the people you're trying to lead.

Some leaders regularly put up the most points and take the big shot with seconds left on the clock. But some leaders are a wise presence in the locker room or in the huddle. You wouldn't know who they were by watching the game on TV—but their teammates know. When I was with the Raptors, one of the leaders we'd look to consistently was Darrick Martin. He never put up the most stats or got the most minutes—but he showed me that you didn't need to do that to lead. He was a consummate professional. He was a steady presence, a veteran who'd been around the league, who made sure the young guys got in their reps in practice and put together team dinners after.

With the Heat, it was Juwan Howard. When I was his teammate, he was nearing the end of his playing career. He didn't play big minutes for us, and in our second championship year he pretty much had a suit on during games the whole year. But he would be in the gym before everybody every single morning. He would hit the treadmill and lift weights every single morning, and get shots up before and after practice every day. And he wasn't even playing. He got it: "I'm not going to play that much, but I'm going to show these guys the amount of work they have to put in to win championships." And he understood that that role needed to be filled. He worked his ass off every single day. You talk about consistency. He is one of the most—if not the most—consistent pros I've ever played with and worked with. He was in there going hard and not even getting any minutes. So there was no excuse for anyone else.

You won't see it on the stat sheet, but every team would be lucky to have a Darrick Martin or a Juwan Howard.

In fact, some of the greatest leaders of all time have led without putting up dominant stats. A few years ago, Sam Walker wrote a book about sports leadership called *The Captain Class*, which identified the traits of leaders on the most successful teams ever to play their sport. "The great captains of these teams were not obvious people," Walker said. "They were rarely stars. They did the grunt work."

For instance, everyone knows about the 1999 U.S. women's soccer team that dominated international competition before winning the World Cup. "Yet if you asked a hundred people who the captain of this team was," Walker pointed out, "odds are none of them would name Carla Overbeck. It's unlikely they would even remember her name—in large part because that's the way she wanted it." Overbeck wasn't the most talented player on the team, but she was a defender who stood out for her passing, her work ethic, and her amazing endurance. She helped players load their bags on and off the bus. She played 3,547 consecutive minutes without coming out of a match, and she once outran all of her teammates—on a broken toe. Overbeck wasn't the flashiest member of that team, but she was arguably the most reliable.

That's what made her the captain. That's why people followed when she led. She didn't have to say anything most of the time. She just had to point. She just had to take the first step and people trusted she knew what was right.

The true test of leadership isn't who puts up the best stats. It's who teammates turn to when things aren't going well. A great leader can pull their team through that. They model the kind of attitude it takes to fix any problem and get a game or a season back on track. Anyone can look like a leader when the shots are falling, when the team looks unbeatable, when you're holding up the trophy. A real leader steps up when things are at their worst.

I remember in my first year in Miami we lost six of seven games coming out of the All-Star break—our first as the Big Three—to begin the stretch run toward the playoffs. We were getting killed in the media. It's like we couldn't do anything right. Things were out of whack. We had the right attitude, but it just seemed like we were in a funk. It all came to a head in a one-point Sunday afternoon home loss to Chicago where we gave up a game we had in the bag with two consecutive bad fouls up two with 25 seconds on the clock and Chicago out of timeouts. The thing is, it wasn't just a bad loss on its own. The Bulls had beaten us a week earlier, and this win on our home floor gave them the season series sweep and propelled them to a 24–4 finish. It also meant they took the No. 1 seed from us. Needless to say, it was a low point and the media was loving it.

The next day at practice, I remember Bron coming in—and you could see it on his face. It wasn't that he wasn't happy. No one was. There was something about him that just *embodied* bouncing back. That he was back on track and we just needed to get on his energy. The intensity that he brought to that practice was inspiring. To see the best player on the court sprinting full speed and leading the team with intensity and effort was what we all needed. We were all diving on the court for loose balls, taking charges, bringing that same intensity to the seemingly mundane drills. Getting back to the basics. That's what a leader does. It's not just hyping the team up when you're winning and everything is comfortable. A leader shows composure when others would fall apart. LeBron didn't need to say anything to get us fired up—he just needed to set the example and trust that we would follow him. And we did. Two months later, we met the Bulls again, this time in the Eastern Conference Finals, and we were a different team. We had no trouble going 4–1, including the clincher on their home floor, where LeBron, D-Wade, and I all went for 20-plus.

Leading by example is a hugely underrated thing. Leading by example is being on time. Demanding that your guys be on time not with nagging or commands but with the power of your presence. I always liked to be dressed and ready to go before practice, so that when the coach blew the whistle, I'd be the first one out on the court, ready to work on my craft. Leading by example means taking care of yourself, eating right, and getting the sleep you need to perform at your peak. Leading by example means setting the level of work ethic you want your teammates to emulate. Leading by example starts with little things like that, repeated day in and day out.

To lead by example, you don't have to bust out a "win one for the Gipper" speech every day. That's a misconception. That's the movies. Communication matters, but not more than showing up and putting in the hours, every damn day. And if you're a quiet personality like me, the few times you really do open your mouth can have a huge impact. I really like something Coach Spoelstra said about me once: "CB knows when to talk, and it's not often. He knows when to push the button." That really made me feel like he got me. I wanted my words to have an impact—and that meant saving them for the right moments. That's the "button" Spo was talking about. If I needed to get in a teammate's face when things were going wrong, I knew that he was going to listen to me, because I only spoke up loudly when there was something really important to say.

But just as not all leaders are the vocal, dominant players, not all leaders are the quiet, lead-by-example types either.

There are the ones who eat tape and absorb playbooks, who can tell you exactly which offensive set is coming in which game situation, who understand your and your opponent's strategy like an extra coach on the floor. There are the QBs, despite a huge contract and a couple of rings, who will call their backup at 2 a.m. to discuss some obscure play buried deep in the playbook. Because they are that committed to winning, because they are still learning. Because they are showing what leadership and dedication look like.

There are the ones who are deeply attuned to the emotional ups and downs of the game—the first ones to pick you up when you've had a bad moment or a bad night, the first ones to celebrate with you when you've hit a personal milestone.

There are the veterans who have been around the block so many times that nothing surprises them—and who pass that calm and wisdom on to the people around them.

And sometimes teams have more than one leader—they have a core of players who each know when it's their turn to step up. In fact, provided that you have a team full of people who are able to tame their egos, I'd say you can never have too many leaders on a team.

Being a leader can be as simple as hosting a party for your teammates, creating time to bond off the court. On the Heat, one of our team rituals was making sure that, on the road, we'd have at least one dinner or breakfast together every day. It didn't matter if we landed at 3 a.m.—we were getting our asses out of bed for breakfast at 10 a.m. Sometimes being a leader can be as simple as being down in the hotel lobby, ready to grab breakfast with the team, even when you'd rather be in bed.

Those are the intangibles that matter so much, even if you don't see them as a fan. But I promise you, you know what a team looks like when they're missing them—dysfunctional, listless, confused. You'd be surprised how common it is when teams don't have that bond—when guys haven't been to each other's houses, don't know the names of each other's kids, don't exchange a word outside the locker room.

Sure, you could say, "It's a business. You're supposed to be coworkers, not friends." And that attitude can work for a while— when things are going well. But when they aren't, when you need to level with one another about what's going wrong and how to fix it, you'll find that teams with that attitude don't have what it takes. Maybe you've heard the expression "Nobody cares what you say until they know how much you care." For the most part, you don't want to listen to someone who treats you as a cog in a machine. Leaders treat their teammates like real people, not cogs—not because they're exceptionally nice, but because they understand that that's how you inspire people to step up.

The ways we consume and experience sports push us in the direction of expecting one-size-fits-all leadership: There is *one* leader, and unless he fits a certain mold at all times, he fails as a leader. But that just doesn't line up with my experience of the game at the highest level. Real life is a lot richer and more complicated. Because the game throws so many different challenges at us, anyone can step up to be a leader when the situation calls for what they have to give. That's not everyone-gets-a-trophy happy talk. It's just realizing that life is a lot more complex than a sports movie, where one big locker room speech turns everything around.

But whichever leadership style fits you, be prepared to change. I can't tell you how many times I've had to change as a leader over the course of my career. I tried to stay true to who I wanted to be as a player others looked up to—to possess qualities like consistency, dependability, competitiveness, positivity. But the specifics of how you're putting those qualities into action are always changing.

Even if you're comfortable in the role you're taking on for your team, the things that are expected of you may change as the situation around you changes. If you feel called to speak up in practice, it doesn't matter if you've been pigeonholed as "the quiet guy." In fact, if you are the quiet guy, the moment you do speak up will be powerful. Because the team will *know* you are serious.

That's one of the things I learned about leadership in Toronto. I learned that leading by example is good, but that sometimes my team needed me to step up and be an emotional leader, too—so I worked really hard on that. The guys knew I didn't just get worked up every day, so if I was heated, it *mattered*.

In Miami, my leadership style had to change again. Now I was part of a Big Three: That meant playing a new role, and sometimes it meant taking a back seat. It would have been easy to get apathetic and just coast, when teammates like D-Wade and LeBron were such established leaders in their own right. But I remembered what Coach Bishop said: Whatever else I did, I could lead by example. And I could show everyone around me that I fully bought into what we were trying to build down there. I trusted that LeBron and D would get me a look if they knew I wanted a shot.

On defense, I made sure I was consistently in the right spots and accepted responsibility for my error if I wasn't. I took pride in being the loudest person on the floor talking on defense, because I could see how keeping everyone on the same page made our defense that much stronger. If I was being the defensive anchor, Bron and D could feel a little more comfortable going for those steals that led to all of those dunks. I wanted my guys to know that I would be where I said I'd be every time. That's how I helped lead in Miami. It was something new for me, but I could see how it contributed to our success as a team.

That's the thing about leadership: It's always changing. And being a leader means being willing to change to meet your team's needs at any given moment. Whoever it is that steps up on any given day, however your leadership style changes over time, being a leader means keeping the ethos of what your team is doing intact. Championship organizations need to have a championship mentality. Leaders keep negativity from seeping in, and they don't let their teammates see them giving in to it.

Being a leader means knowing your teammates, speaking to each one of them, letting them know that they all matter. But how many of us can really get past our egos and know our teammates on a meaningful level? That's why leadership is hard—it means breaking out of your shell and your comfort zone when you don't necessarily want to.

Leaders also model what it looks like to be a good follower. They can take orders and instruction from the coach, or from other teammates. They can show their teammates what it looks like to set ego aside.

Leaders motivate their teammates, by words or actions, even when they don't feel like it. They do it when times are tough—in the middle of a shooting slump or a losing streak. They're ready to bear the brunt of criticism, because they are self-confident enough to take it. And sometimes that means being exposed to unfair criticism. Leaders get over it.

Leaders aren't infallible. Part of what gives them the credibility to call their teammates out is their willingness to admit when they're wrong. When I was with the Heat in 2015, I remember having a heated exchange with Coach Spoelstra during a road game in Utah. I'd had some tough days in a row off the court, and I let it spill onto the court. I could tell I said some things that he didn't care for during that exchange. It's a part of the game. You get emotional sometimes, and sometimes it just gets the best of you. We ended up losing the game, and it was especially frustrating because we were heading into Golden State afterward. It was a missed opportunity. No one was happy.

But Spo knew that he couldn't just let something like that go. As a leader of the team, it was his job to make sure we resolved the issue. And because I was a team leader, too, I had to model a better attitude for my teammates, even when things were tough. Before practice the next day, Spo and I had breakfast. We talked it out and came up with a plan for how to move forward. He could have just let things get awkward and fester—but instead, he took the more difficult route of actually working on our issues. So we hashed it out over some eggs and went to practice. Before the next film session, I stood up in front of the team and apologized for what I'd done.

I'd be lying if I said it was easy—admitting you made a mistake never is. But as a leader, I knew it was my job to address the elephant in the room. I knew that that was part of the definition of leadership, too: If you want to call people out on their mistakes, be prepared to own up to yours. And Spo made it easier, because he talked things out with me man-to-man instead of letting things spiral into some sort of grudge. Both of us cared about winning more than anything, both of us knew that we'd only succeed if the other succeeded, too, and that helped us get over our pride.

That's another thing Coach Bishop told me when I was starting out: Teams have a collective spirit, a collective soul. Leaders are in touch with that spirit, and they know how to keep it positive. Even the greatest leaders know they're part of something bigger than themselves.

And just as leaders are part of something bigger than themselves, the idea of leadership is bigger than you think it is—bigger than a lot of people will tell you. If you think that the ultimate leader is going to walk through the door, or if you think you're not cut out to be a leader because you don't fit some stereotype you have in your head, you're making a big mistake. Don't wait on that person. Don't wait to be that person. Don't wait for that supreme leader who's going to show you the way, or give you all the knowledge in the secret scrolls, or whatever you think it is. Most of the time, that person doesn't exist.

But you do. Your skills are real. Your will to win is real. Your leadership potential is real. It's up to you to figure out how to use it.

Wherever your team is—whether it's a rec league squad or a team at the highest level, whether you're coming off a championship or a winless season—your team needs a leader. Every team does. And everyone has it in them to step up to the moment and offer the leadership their team needs. The leader your team needs right now can be you.

# TAKE CARE OF YOURSELF

Playing alongside LeBron James means that I had the privilege of watching one of the greatest players in the history of our sport up close. A lot of what I saw wasn't that different from what the fans saw watching on TV. But I also got to see behind the scenes. I got to see the discipline and routines that, in addition to his talent, built LeBron.

That's important because we tend to think that heroes are *born* rather than made. We also forget, as far as athletes go, that it's not just about getting in shape, but *staying* in shape. That no one can be great, consistently, without figuring out how to maintain and protect their body.

Being part of the team in Miami was a blast. I was an equal among peers. We got to hang out a lot, playing cards and staying up late every night, sometimes going out and having legendary parties.

But one thing that is seared in my memory from those early days is watching LeBron stretch. He had a thirty-minute stretching routine, and he told me he stretched every day when he woke up in the morning and then again before going to bed at night. And that's on top of stretching before and after workouts, practices, and games. I've seen LeBron get up from card games to make sure he got his stretches in. How many times did I see him stretch? A thousand? More?

If you've never been around an NBA locker room, I can tell you: Everyone stretches. But LeBron's commitment to stretching is, by comparison with everyone else in the league, way over the top. He said that he was inspired by a coach early in his playing days who told him, "All that dunking is great, but if you want to keep doing that, you need to stretch." He took it to heart . . . and we mostly laughed at it. On top of that, LeBron has been icing his knees thirty minutes each day since high school.

I had heard since I was a teenager that I should stretch, too. But when you're young, you don't think about it. Because your body is so supple, so resilient that you can treat it like garbage and not even know what you're doing to it. When I was young I wasn't thinking about prolonging my career. I wasn't thinking about improving my recovery time. I wasn't thinking about regrets when I got older. Man, I wasn't sure I *would* ever be old. My mentality was "hoop and go home." I was taking it day by day, pushing through the pain, acting like I was going to be young forever. Get there early to stretch before the game? Stay late to stretch after? Who had the time?

In high school, my buddies and I were eating Quarter Pounders before every game. And we were not alone. For a long time, the most popular restaurant among NFL players was the Cheesecake Factory. Lots of options, big portions, big booths, lots of calories, at a decent price. Who plays in the NFL? A bunch of huge guys in their midtwenties.

I grew out of my Quarter Pounder habit—which my dad used to say was like "putting regular gas in a Ferrari"—but a lot of athletes still have that same mentality, or something like it.

Don't get me wrong—I love ice cream, I love Snickers bars, I love Quarter Pounders. And it's not like I swore off those things entirely. It's that I learned how to enjoy them in moderation, because I'd rather skip a few ice creams and win a championship than eat whatever I want whenever I want and never maximize my potential.

True, you can go pretty far in your career while doing the minimum to take care of yourself. But the true greats—the ones who sustain greatness year after year, the LeBrons and the Tom Bradys—put in something extra. In Miami, it was eye-opening for me to see Dwyane and LeBron take care of their bodies. They were the ones who got me to see that my body was my asset. Ray Allen, too, since he was almost ten years older, was always talking about new treatments, therapies, anything to get that edge to be able to recover a little quicker. Sooner or later, that difference is going to make itself felt on the court, and it's going to be the single biggest factor in the number of seasons you'll be able to play at an elite level.

Think of it this way: If you owned a factory, the building and the machines inside it would be your capital, the things you own that let you make money by producing whatever it is the factory makes. If you took some of your profits and invested them back into the factory—by buying new machines, or by repairing the ones that broke down—you'd be able to go on making money. If you invested in more-efficient machines, maybe you'd even be able to make more money than before. But if you neglected those investments, the machines would eventually get old and break down, and one day you'd be out of business.

If you're an athlete, the closest thing you have to that factory is your own body. It's the capital that allows you to excel at your sport—and, given all we know about how connected the mind and body are, at other areas of life, too. If you're a pro, investing in that asset is a strategy that literally pays off monetarily. But if you're not, investing in your body still makes a difference—the difference between knowing that you're performing at your peak and wondering if you left something on the table. In either case, your body is your greatest asset as an athlete. You have to protect it. You have to invest in it. If you don't, the value of that asset is guaranteed to decline over time.

They say athletes are genetic freaks, and maybe to some extent we are. But that doesn't change the fact that every league is filled with guys and gals who are all genetically blessed. You're competing against folks who have also been gifted by the gods. So if you're not putting in the work, if you're not respecting the gift?

Man, it will not last.

If you're not putting in the investment, you can be assured that someone you compete against is. This isn't the Babe Ruth days, where your opponent is also going to house a dozen hot dogs, smoke a cigarette, and then suit up to play. Standards change, and the science behind taking care of your mind and body is getting better every year. If you don't keep up, other people who do are going to leave you behind.

A few years ago, Bill Simmons was talking on a podcast about a conversation he had with LeBron's business partner, Maverick Carter. And Simmons was just blown away by hearing about all of the time, effort, and money—Carter estimated it at $1.5 million a year—that LeBron puts into maintaining his body. It's everything from hiring personal chefs and masseuses, to optimizing his sleep habits, to building a home gym that replicates his team's training facilities.

That sounds insane, unless you see it like he does, as an investment in staying on top of his sport. Taking it just in monetary terms, LeBron wouldn't be able to pull down tens of millions in salary and endorsements year after year if he didn't keep himself in prime condition. In financial terms, and of course in terms of his success on the court, investing so much in taking care of his body absolutely pays off.

If you ever wonder how a guy like LeBron stays so durable for so long, there's your answer. It's the same answer that explains how F1 cars can go so fast and Thoroughbred horses can endure the punishment of race after race.

Again, genetics play a part—but only a part. Sure, talent plays a part—but only a part. The other part, and by far the bigger one, is the science. It's the time and effort that goes into taking care of the valuable asset.

Taking care of your body—your machine—is a science. LeBron is durable because he works at being durable. The effort he puts into taking care of his body is just as great as the effort he puts into his post moves or his jumper. You think he hasn't read books about this? That he doesn't ask for advice? That he hasn't been keeping his eyes open and learning about this science for the last two decades? The mind is a muscle and it serves the other muscles.

In the Finals, LeBron would have to play 40-plus minutes a night at full speed, then jump on a cross-country flight, then do it all over again less than forty-eight hours later. In a report a few years ago on his recovery routine during his second stint with Cleveland, when he went up against the Warriors in the Finals, a fitness expert said that the closest sports analogy he could think of for what LeBron was putting his body through was the Tour de France, the famously grueling bike race. LeBron's recovery routine started right after game time with recovery drinks, protein, and carbs, as well as immersion in an ice bath, which he calls "borderline torture." On the flight, he'd keep pounding recovery drinks, and he'd get massages and electro stimulation. And then, according to Cork Gaines of *Business Insider*, it kept going:

The flight from San Francisco lands back in Cleveland at 6:30 a.m. At this point, James goes home for some sleep and then heads back at the team's training facility at 1 p.m.

With about 30 hours to go before tip-off, James works out on a stationary bike and treats his body with contrasting hot and cold baths.

Two hours later, James is back home where he is met by his personal trainer, Mike Mancias . . . The two go through four hours of "treatment, massage, and rehab."

The thing is, that's a facet of the game that fans rarely see. They see us hitting warmup shots in sweats before the game, and then jogging out onto the court for tip-off like it's an ordinary day at the office for a professional. They see us running up and down the court for a couple of hours, and that seems hard enough. But we don't just show up to the game like some people show up for work. If it's a seven o'clock game, we show up at four o'clock, five latest. I want to be on the court getting my shots up at least two hours before tip-off. Some came earlier. Ray usually got to the gym around three!

And then after the game, there's icing, treatment, tending to whatever on your body happens to be hurting that day. You were just out there damaging your body, so you need to consult with the trainers and start the healing—and that's another couple of hours after the whistle, win or lose.

When you're on the road, you take that shit with you, too. It's not like you leave the game, hit the shower, and hit the club. This isn't the clock-in, clock-out life. It doesn't matter what the players' union rules say, you stay until you've done what you need to do. Did you turn your ankle or jam your finger or get a bruise? That's extra work. And if you're really taking care of your body, you're doing extra stretching and weight training and diet monitoring at home, too.

To take another example of one of the greats, you've probably heard about all of the effort Tom Brady puts into keeping himself in excellent shape, which has helped him play at the highest level into his forties. He's as fanatical as LeBron about stretching and body pliability. But it starts with diet. As Julia Belluz wrote for *Vox:*

> Brady eats a mostly organic, local, and plant-based diet with no highly processed foods. In the morning, he starts with 20 ounces of "water with electrolytes," then a fruit smoothie, and after working out, more water and a protein shake. Lunch is typically fish and vegetables. Afternoon snacks consist of fruits, protein bars, and more protein shakes; dinners include more vegetables and sometimes soup broth.
>
> Even more notable than what Brady eats is what he doesn't. He avoids alcohol, as well as gluten-containing bread and pasta, breakfast cereal, corn, dairy, foods that contain GMOs, high-fructose corn

syrup, trans fats, sugar, artificial sweeteners, soy, fruit juice, grain-based foods, jams and jellies, most cooking oils, frozen dinners, salty snacks, sugary snacks, sweetened drinks, white potatoes, and prepackaged condiments like ketchup and soy sauce.

Now, Brady has some pretty intense beliefs about what is and isn't OK to eat—apparently he doesn't even touch tomatoes. It works for him, and the commitment and ritual of it is probably a big part of why.

I can tell you with more certainty that you won't go wrong eating mostly fruits and vegetables and staying away from processed foods. And I can tell you that there's no way you get to Brady-like longevity without being as deliberate as he is about diet, nutrition, and exercise.

I've tried to learn from people like that. I don't think my own investments in my body and health ever got to the seven-figure level, but after seeing how careful guys like LeBron, Dwyane, and Ray were about their bodies, I started to take self-care more seriously. Up through the Toronto phase of my career, it was mostly an afterthought, mostly because the NBA hadn't really come around yet on taking durability and self-care seriously. Those things were for the old guys trying to eke out a few more years. If you were a youngster like I was, even talking about them was taboo. I remember that if you were a young guy getting extra work in on the massage tables, veterans would say things like, "You're young, you don't need that."

Now that sounds like the craziest shit you ever heard! "You're young, you don't need to take care of your body." But that was the culture when I was coming up. Even then, it sounded crazy to me.

Still, coming to Miami with D and Bron, and watching how much they put into the game, it made me think, "Damn, I haven't done any of this stuff." But mainly it was about athletes treating the game and their bodies as seriously as they deserved to be treated. It was about extending your peak performance as far as possible—so that it's not just a year or two when your body is at its sharpest, but the majority of your career. Doing things like hiring a personal chef, creating routines for stretching, icing, massages—they were some of the best decisions I made in my career.

One of the biggest things I added late in my career was a mindfulness routine at the end of the evening, so I could put aside the distractions of the day and get some solid sleep. I do things like close my eyes and practice breathing exercises, or wind down by reading a book. All of that helps your body get to sleep as soon as your head hits the pillow, and that's essential, because sleep is crucial to the body's recovery. In recent years, I've heard from more and more athletes who have a "no screens in the bedroom" rule, because they know that you can't mess with sleep any more than you can mess with your diet.

The important thing to realize about taking care of yourself is that it's something no one else can do for you, because no one else has the stake in it that you do. Sure, coaches and trainers tell you things like, "You need to add muscle if you want to bang down low in the post." I got those messages, and I took them really seriously. Sometimes, adding muscle seemed even more important than the actual games. But you work out one way if you want to get immediate gains, and you work out another way if you want to keep your body durable for the long haul of a career. It wasn't until later in my career that I realized the difference. And it wasn't until later in my career that I realized that no one—not coaches, not trainers, not teammates—is as invested in your long-term durability as you are yourself.

You want to be knowledgeable about your body. Remember, it's the main tool of your trade. Would you trust a carpenter or a plumber who couldn't explain every tool in his toolbox to you? It's the same with athletes. You need to be able to advocate for yourself with doctors, trainers, and coaches. I'm not saying you shouldn't trust them—just that you're the only one who can provide reliable information about how your body is doing at any given moment, and you need to learn how to monitor that information and communicate it confidently.

Think about Kawhi Leonard—when he hurt his right quad in the 2017–18 season, he chose to sit out and rehab for the remainder of the season, even though everyone in San Antonio was convinced that he could get back on the court sooner. But Kawhi was adamant that he was not going to play until his body felt ready, even if it meant getting traded to Toronto. You know what happened next—when he *was* ready to get back on the court, he led his new team to a championship. Would things have played out differently if he had listened to the Spurs organization and shortened his rehab? Who knows? Maybe he would have been fine; maybe he would have suffered a career-ending injury. The point is that Kawhi was the only person in the world who knew how his body was feeling—and he made his call and stuck with it.

And this is a long way from how players used to act, smoking in the locker room, playing through injuries, gaining lots of weight in the off-season. It shouldn't surprise us that the quality of play has gotten better and better through the decades, and careers have gotten longer. It's because athletes are respecting themselves and their assets.

Taking care of your body isn't just about eating right, sleeping right, and working out. It's about learning how to listen to your body, knowing when exhaustion is something you can push through, and knowing when you genuinely have to shut your body down to let it recover. That's all that the "load management" you hear so much about in today's NBA means. It's about players and coaches putting more value on durability and on sustaining peak performance. And it's about athletes getting more sophisticated in understanding their bodies and how to advocate for their long-term health.

Yes, a while ago, I told you about how important it is to know when to ignore your body's "distress signals" and push through the pain.* And yeah, that's part of being an elite athlete. But so is understanding when to shut it down and let your body recover. How do you know the difference? Well, for the most part, you just *know*. If you practice hard enough, and get enough experience in pushing yourself up to and past your limits, you'll know what "tired and sore" feels like. And if you do that, you'll also know what "legitimately hurt" feels like. Anyone who's played enough knows the difference, even if they can't put it into words. And the more you push yourself, the more you care for and learn about your body, the better you'll be able to spot it. Most of all, you'll have the *confidence* to stand up for yourself when you're really hurting. You won't have that little voice in your head asking if you're really just tired—because you'll have experience with playing through that.

When I hear about NFL players covering up their concussion symptoms so they can get back on the field, or about players in any sport who get hooked on painkillers so they can play through an injury, I just feel for those guys. Part of it is the economics of sports—the fact that so many teams treat guys, especially non-superstars, as disposable, so players face the choice between play-

---

* It's worth saying here that taking care of your *mental* health is essential, too. I salute the awareness that Kevin Love and other players are bringing to this issue. It doesn't matter whether you're in great physical shape; depression, anxiety, harmful thoughts—they can upend your life and career worse than any injury. So don't play through them or ignore them. Get help. Take it seriously. You deserve to feel good inside.

ing through injury and getting cut. But the other part of it is that we athletes have to help each other learn to advocate for ourselves, to say, "I know what sore feels like, and I know what injured feels like—and what I'm feeling right now isn't just sore." That's what self-care is really about. It isn't about going to the spa and soaking in a hot tub. It's about saying, "If I don't prioritize my well-being, who will?"

I know why neglecting your body at times can be such a temptation. The problem is that our bodies always betray us sooner or later. And if you don't take care of your body when you're in peak form, it's a lot like charging everything to your credit card. Sooner or later, the bill is going to come due, and it's going to be huge.

But the good news is that with hard work and commitment, you can pay it. In the 2018–19 season, Warriors GM Bob Myers pulled Draymond Green aside one day and told him that if the Warriors were going to keep their position at the top of the league and the conference, he needed to lose something like thirty pounds. Can you imagine that? He did it, though. Draymond cut everything bad out of his diet, lost the weight, and returned to form by the time the playoffs rolled around. And despite two catastrophic injuries to two of their three best players, the Warriors still almost won the title again, in no small part because Draymond was healthy enough to do that thing that he does.

Conditioning is something we have to do every year. No amount of past victories or experience affords you the luxury of being out of shape. That's the profession we chose. It's a tough one.

Now, you've probably guessed that there's a big irony here. I've spent all this time telling you about durability—and I spent all of the time in my career working to make my body more durable—and yet my career came to an end because of a medical issue I couldn't control. I wasn't able to play into my forties, or to be a contributor on a championship team well into the twilight of my career. In one sense, I wasn't able to reap the rewards of all the work I put into maintaining my body. So was it all a waste?

No, I don't think so. We can't control everything that happens to us—I couldn't control my blood clots, for instance. But we can still take pride in what we *do* control.

I'm proud that I took the game seriously enough to give my all to it as long as I could, on the court and off, even if it meant passing up a few Snickers bars.

I'm proud that I learned how to take ownership of my body and my health, in a way that few young players were being encouraged to do when I came into the league.

I'm proud that my body is still healthy and that my mind will be sharp for decades to come.

Remember that saying, *Mens sana in corpore sano*? It means "a sound mind in a sound body." Your mind is part of your body. I care about being at peak mental performance for as long as I possibly can be—and if you're reading this book, I'm pretty sure that you care about that, too. Take it from me: You don't get peak mental performance without taking care of your body.

Sleeping right. Eating right. Exercising. Those investments in yourself don't stop paying off when you stop playing the game—they will pay dividends for your whole life.

So put that work into yourself, and be proud of it. None of it is ever wasted.

# LETTER 9

# DON'T LET 'EM GET TO YOU

t would be wonderful if you could just play ball and be left alone, but the better you get at this game—or really, the better you get at anything in life—the less possible that is.

With talent and skill and success comes the inevitability of criticism. Maybe you've heard the saying that "criticism is a tax on success." In my experience, it's absolutely true. And that means two things. First, like a tax, there's no way out of paying the bill. It would be great if you only got positive attention for your success. It would feel fairer, too, wouldn't it? After all, you're the one who's putting in the work, you're the one who's hitting the gym when the haters are logging hours on Xbox, and it would be wonderful if they had some more humility about that. They could pat you on the back when you have a good game. And when you have a bad one? Before they decided to put more negativity out into the world, they could take a deep breath and reconsider.

But, of course, that's not going to happen. Criticism is a tax you pay, and it always comes due. Better to accept that now—just like businesses budget in the amount of tax they have to pay each year—than to act shocked every time you see the bill.

There's another side of that statement: Criticism is a tax on *success*. If you're getting criticized, even unfairly, take a second to appreciate it—it means you're doing something right. It means you're winning more than you're losing. It means you're attracting attention. No one criticizes the underdog, the eight-seed, the perennial loser. What's the point in that? Beating up on a team or a player who's down big is just mean and pointless—that's why Little League has the "mercy rule." If you're attracting enough attention to also attract criticism, don't let that get you down—enjoy it. You've earned it.

What does it mean if you have a huge tax bill? It means *you made a lot of money*. I've paid my share of big bills on signing bonuses and endorsement deals over the years, and it stings . . . but only because the blessing is so big.

Only a fool complains about the bad that comes with the good. Being hit with criticism means you're *doing something in this life*. It means people care, that you register in their lives. It means your actions have impact.

I wish you much success and happiness in life, but you have to know that this success is not going to make everyone around you happy. Not everyone is rooting for you like I am or like your parents are. That's just a sad fact of life. Every champion in NBA history, even the teams with the biggest bandwagons, had millions of people rooting for them to fail. People *enjoyed* seeing them lose—in part because it was so rare. The Warriors went 73–9 in 2015–16, which meant at least nine games people were very happy to see them painfully lose. And what about the 2019–20 season? From one of the best records in the league . . . to the worst. Even shortened, the season was awful for them.

Haters were ecstatic. We like to watch people at the top fall from their heights. It makes us feel good about ourselves.

The bigger you are, the more you get second-guessed—whether it's a handful of jerks jumping into your Instagram, or the national media raking you over the coals. The more you do, the higher the expectations placed on you, and the higher the standard you're held to. No one's criticizing a high school freshman for not playing at an NBA level. But every time that freshman excels at his current level and shows glimpses of the next one, he's raising the bar for himself. Some of the criticism he'll get will be from teammates and coaches who genuinely want him to get better—who are frustrated with him when he dogs it on an off day at practice, because they know he's got more in him than that. Some of the criticism he'll get will just be from people who envy his success. But the rule holds: the more success, the higher the bar, the more criticism.

At the far end of the scale, who do you think the most criticized player in the NBA is? It's not some twelfth man or rookie—it's guys like LeBron and KD.

No one gets out of it, not even the greats. Like feeling your body break down at the end of a long season, it's just one of the occupational hazards of the game. But just as some players are better than others at pushing through pain, some players are better than others at pushing through criticism—keeping the critiques that matter, so they can keep improving their game, and tuning out the rest. A big part of being great is how well you bear that burden. Because, one way or another, you're going to have to bear it. If you want to be successful, you're going to have to get used to it. You're going to have to use the criticism to make you stronger.

It doesn't just matter for your success on the court or on the field. It matters for the kind of person you want to become. Some people get so consumed with bitterness that criticism takes all the joy out of success. Other people tune it out so much that they get arrogant, convinced they have nothing to learn. A few people make it to the sweet spot, handling criticism with grace, learning from it where they can, but not getting consumed by it. Those people are usually the most successful of all—but more importantly, they're the most content with themselves.

I've tried to get to that balanced place—self-confident enough to shake off the dumb criticism, humble enough to learn from the smart criticism—for most of my career. But it took me longer than some of my peers, who have been under the microscope almost their whole lives. I was a bit sheltered by comparison. Toronto before Drake wasn't as popular and didn't get as much notoriety in the United States.

But still, I knew what it was like to be screamed at by fans. When I played in Toronto, we were the only NBA team *in the entire country*, so there was a spotlight on us at all times. And then in Miami, it was like a whole other world—from the day LeBron and I signed and joined forces with D-Wade, we were the biggest focus of attention, hate, and criticism in the league. That took some adjustment.

It wasn't just the hate I got from fans and random people on social media. It was from some former players, too. Old-school guys like Chuck and Oak and Scottie would say stuff about all three of us like, "I would never *join* those other two guys, I would try to *beat* them." Or they'd make it much simpler: "MJ would never do that." I'll admit it, it got to me. Here I was, averaging eight rebounds, almost 19 points per game, and I just felt like shit sometimes. I felt like I deserved the criticism. The worst part was knowing that even though I changed my team, I hadn't changed as a player. I was still hitting the gym, still attacking the game humbly, still working to mesh with my teammates. Getting caught up in a media-driven narrative like that can be shocking if it's never happened to you before. You feel the same on the inside, and yet suddenly you're the bad guy. And maybe this sounds dumb in retrospect, but it really blindsided me—I thought people were going to *love* watching us play. Oops.

I saw all of that criticism. "Bosh Spice." "Fake tough guy." *Bleacher Report* ran a series called "Everybody Hates Chris." Man, wtf?

I let a lot of that criticism penetrate my psyche—and it was mentally exhausting. I wanted to act like it never got to me—but of course it got to me. I'm human, and any human who tells you criticism doesn't ever faze them is either lying or a sociopath. When you're getting criticized as constantly as the Heat were in those days, you start looking over your shoulder even as you're playing the games, second-guessing the shots you took or didn't take, wondering what you're going to tell the reporters if you lose the game, while there's still time on the clock.

Things that used to be fun for me, like messing around on social media, got to be a huge drag. Instead of unwinding, I'd just waste time thinking, *Why are people so angry? Why do they have to be jerks to a guy they've never met?* And it sounds naive to say now, but one of the things that got to me the most was the fact that a lot of it wasn't about basketball. It wasn't just that I was supposed to be a bad player—it was that I was supposed to be a bad person, too. People talk about your family, your kids, your wife. So much of that stuff felt like it was meant to turn players against each other, or turn us against our coaching staff, or just make us feel miserable for the hell of it. Worrying about that stuff is destructive, and it wastes so much energy.

At first I didn't understand it, and it led to quite a bit of resentment. I didn't understand that being a target of criticism was part of what I'd signed up for. It just seemed like people were going out of their way to mess with me—like the more I tried to tune them out, the louder they became. The game stopped being fun. I played angry. I wanted to win to spite people. It was a bad place. I was getting far from the *why* I should have been playing the game for.

After we lost in the Finals to Dallas, there were days when I didn't want to leave my house. The whole team was depressed. But I had to come to terms with something about criticism— something that more-scrutinized players realize a lot earlier in their careers: It was always going to be there. More to the point, my choice to join the Heat—as happy as I was with the decision, and as much as it made sense from a basketball and a life perspective—was going to make me the villain for the average NBA fan. I just wasn't going to get that fan love, no matter how much I felt entitled to it.

But you know what? Realizing that was an enormous relief. I stopped looking over my shoulder. I stopped apologizing for my choices. I cut way back on the amount of time I spent reading about my team and the league, and I read stuff that was more rewarding instead. That's something I say to guys now. Time spent on Twitter is time *not* spent reading books. What do you mean you don't have time to read or stretch or connect with your teammates? Of course you have the time—you're just spending it in the wrong places.

What I learned to do was to start putting more energy into

making myself happy, and into being the best teammate I could be. I worked actively to let go of the expectation that everyone should love me. It was transformative. Energy that was previously going into making me miserable was now making me better—as a person and as a player.

And my teammates helped me through it. The next year, there was an unspoken agreement that we weren't going to complain and whine about criticism together, no matter how unfair it was. We were just going to collectively tune it out and work at being champions. Hate is only a topic of conversation if you let it become one. We stopped playing to shut the haters up, and we started playing for ourselves.

Even if you never have to play on a team that's cast as the villain—whether for your local league, or for the whole NBA—I think you can learn something from my experience here. The best way to cope with criticism is to come to terms with its inevitability.

Does anybody actually *like* criticism? Of course not. In all my days playing, I don't think I ever met a player who really liked it when Coach was getting on him. Nobody pulls up Twitter and is happy to hear people talking trash, just like no player gets excited for the press conference after a loss. If you can't stand people coming after you for your perceived faults and failures, you've got company.

But there's a big difference between not liking criticism and imagining that with the right game, the right comeback, the right

PR, you can make criticism go away. Once you realize that you can't—that the more successful you get, the more the criticism will be amplified—you may be able to reach some kind of peace with it. That was my experience. It wasn't "proving the haters wrong" that helped me get over criticism. It was realizing that *nothing* I could do would prevent me from paying the tax, so I might as well start budgeting for it.

You just cannot take seriously every single negative word you hear about yourself. I'd see that all the time in college and the NBA—young guys overwhelmed because there was just so much criticism. *Didn't you see your teammate open in the corner on the last play? Why don't you hit more free throws? Why don't you fix your jump shot?* It's those voices in your head we talked about before. It's there in every sport. High school quarterbacks who have the whole town telling them how to throw. Chess champions with overbearing parents. Talented veterans at the end of their careers who have to hear *SportsCenter* anchors calling for their retirement, saying that they lost it.

Sometimes people just want to get a rise out of you. People like that know that they're never going to be successful, they're never going to win championships—but if they taunt you and you react, then just for that moment, they have power over you, and that feels good to them. "Bro, did you see how mad he got when I told him he sucked?" Or worse, sometimes you'll hear some broken people say some racist stuff, say some cruel stuff. Why?

I wish I knew. All I can tell you is that it doesn't have anything to do with you. All I can tell you is that as bad as those remarks make you feel, I promise you, it is darker and more painful inside that person's heart.

I'll be honest, there have been times when I wanted to run up into the stands and start something with guys like that. But I've always held myself back—because the minute you stoop to their level, that's when you're giving them power over you. Part of playing at the highest level is knowing that lots of eyes are on you, and that you have to act accordingly.

So most of the criticism you hear as an athlete can be safely tuned out. Free advice is usually worth what you pay for it. The more you learn to do a better job separating the signal from the noise, the more you're equipped to deal with the urgent (and still painful) criticism that does matter.

What people are saying on social media—you can tune that out. What some random kid on the third row of bleachers is yelling at you during an open practice? Not important. Your dad who left when you were three but comes back into your life when you're starting to show promise and is now acting like he's always been in your corner? That's something you want to be wary of. The same goes for your opponent who is trash talking you, trying to get in your head. That's why I tried to stop reading about myself when I was playing in the league, whether it was good or bad. It might puff me up with pride or depress me, depending on the day, but the one thing I knew it wouldn't do was help me sharpen my craft. And whenever I picked up on some of the noise, I'd just remind myself: "Michael Jordan got criticized! In the middle of his second three-peat, people were saying he was too old. If he got criticized, you're getting criticized. Think about how much crap Shaq and Kobe got during their run. It's nothing new. Get over it."

If you're playing a team sport, you can say the same thing about criticism that focuses on you as an individual rather than as a member of a team. Team sports are complicated, and winning or losing rarely comes down to one guy. If someone says that a loss was all your fault—even if you did screw up in a big moment—that's a good sign that they're pretty ignorant about the game. Similarly, if someone tries to puff you up by saying you need to get your 25 points regardless of how your teammates are playing, that's another sign that they don't know much about what team sports are all about.

And the media? You can tune that out, too. Understand that their job isn't to make us better players—it's to tell stories, get clicks, and generate attention. That doesn't mean that the media is your enemy, and it doesn't mean you have to take a paranoid, hostile stance toward journalists. It just means that they have different incentives than you do. And most of the time, it's the simple stories, with clear-cut heroes and villains, that garner the most attention. You don't have a lot of control over which box you get sorted into. So don't take it personally. Recognize that the media is playing its game on top of yours, and that they are two very separate endeavors. And remember what the Stoic philosopher Zeno said: "Better to trip with the feet than with the tongue." In other words, you can't unsay anything—so think before you speak, and don't be ashamed about being quiet.

But once you filter all of the noise out, you're left with the criticism that matters. That's the other side of it. Once you realize that you can't make the criticism stop, you can start perfecting your techniques for sorting the valuable kind from the worthless kind. For instance, a big part of every coach's job is criticism—and the great coaches are especially good at criticizing constructively. What good is a coach who doesn't tell you where you're falling short and where you have to do better? *That's their job.*

As you mature as a player, you start to realize that some—not all, but some—criticism is like that. Listening to it can make you better. And the more mature you get, the more you are able to separate the noise from the criticism that helps you grow. You learn that it's a mistake to write off all criticism as the jealousy of "haters." If you tune it all out, you're basically choosing to freeze your growth and development right at that point.

Listening to criticism the right way takes intelligence. It takes cultivating your mind, just like we talked about earlier. You can't be passive. You can't let it wash over you. You have to *think.* Is this critique valid? Who's giving it to me? What are their motives? What's their relationship with me? If it's a good critique, how can I act on it to become a better player?

Filtering out pointless criticism is a lot like filtering where you get your news. Always ask yourself, "What's the source? Can I trust it?" I started narrowing down my list of trusted sources to people I knew had my best interests at heart—family, close friends, teammates, coaches, trainers. Just as importantly, I encouraged the people I *did* trust to be honest with me. I listened, even when what they said hurt my pride. I didn't lash out, or walk away, or sulk. In that way, I cultivated an inner circle of people who could be honest with me about the shortcomings in my game, but who I also trusted weren't criticizing just to criticize.

Think about this book. If it's any good, in part it's good because I sent it to people I trust, people with different experiences than mine, and asked: How could it be better? Where is it weak? What didn't you like? I didn't listen to all their feedback, but I took a lot of it. They made the final product better.

Great players think critically about criticism all the time. Great *anythings* do. As I've been working on these letters over the past few months, I came across a saying: "If someone tells you something's wrong about your writing, they're right. If they tell you how to fix it, they're often wrong." What that means to me is that writing something like these letters is all about explaining what's in my head in a way that will make sense to you, the person reading it. If a reader doesn't get what I'm trying to say, for whatever reason, that's on me—it's my job to explain things more clearly. But at the same time, just because someone can point out to you a paragraph or a sentence that doesn't make sense, that doesn't mean they know how to fix it.

The philosopher Aristotle said something similar a long time ago: You don't have to be a shoemaker to know if the shoe you're wearing hurts your foot. In other words, being able to identify a problem isn't the same as being able to solve it—and, putting it the other way around, people who don't have solutions can still give you valuable information on where the problems are. Identifying problems and solving them are both important—but we also have to keep them separate in our minds.

There aren't any blanket answers here. Think about coaches again. Like I said, coaches are usually trying to help the team win, just like your teammates. But they aren't flawless—no one is. Some coaches are just mad when things don't go perfectly—but hey, it's an imperfect game. Other coaches are insecure, and so they criticize you for deviating from the plan—but again, you're the one on the court. Others—the kind anyone is lucky to play for—criticize because they want to build you up into a better player, not because they want to make themselves feel bigger. Some of the greatest coaches hardly ever raise their voice. Think about Phil Jackson, the great coach of the Bulls and Lakers. How often did you see him yelling?

As you grow, you don't just have to figure out how to take criticism—if you want to be a leader, you have to give it, too. Just as with coaches, that's a huge part of the job description of being a team leader—someone who calls out his teammates when they need to be called out, not to break them down or make himself feel better, but to build them up as players.

Great leaders don't just hand out compliments all the time—they push the people around them. But they do it on the basis of respect, and of the relationship that's already there. You're going to be a lot more receptive to what I have to say if I just took a hard screen for you—because that shows I'm willing to put my ass on the line to help us win. And you're going to be a lot more receptive to what I have to say if I show you I recognize the good things you're doing, too. You've probably heard of the "compliment sandwich": If you have to criticize someone, sandwich it between two nice things so it goes down more easily. You don't have to use that formula every time, but the idea is that recognizing the good as well as the bad makes you a lot more credible.

When you do get criticized, whether or not the criticism is valid or spiteful, it's going to sting either way. It could sting in a good way, because it's prodding you to get better, or it could just sting in the way all pointless cruelty does. But it's still going to hurt. And when it does, there's one way to get it out of your head: Get into the gym, and fall into your craft. Anytime I had trouble with criticism, that's how I'd respond. *Teammate had a bad shooting night and took it out on me?* That's more reps on the bench press. *Idiot dragging me on Twitter?* That's a hundred practice free throws. And so on. I didn't do it angrily. I did it with a smile. I did it because I loved the game.

It was always helpful to remind myself that when people criticize me, it's just words—but what I do on the court, or in the gym, is action.

When I went back to the critical comments, I tried to do so deliberately, with discipline. I'd ask myself: Will taking this comment seriously make me better? Will it get me closer to the best I can be as a player? If that's the case, I'm open to it. Even if they're being mean. Even if they're on the opposing team. Even if I'd wish it weren't true. Not just open to it, *hungry* for it. Every great player is.

More than that, every great player is their own harshest critic. They *know* when criticism is on target, because they're sharp students of the game themselves. And when it is on target, they own it. That's how I tried to be. In 2013, when we were in the Eastern Conference Finals against Indiana, I was not playing well and, man, I was *hearing* about it. Going into Game 7, I decided I was going to step up. I went to the reporters and, before anybody could criticize me, took it on myself to apologize to the fans of Miami and to my coaches and to my team. I said, "Let's get this out of the way: I've sucked the last couple games. Nobody is more aware of that than me. I'm gonna fix it." People were shocked by the honesty, and by the ownership. It lifted a huge weight off me and the team. And it took power away from the people who were criticizing just to bring me down a notch. When I got out on the court that night, I felt lighter. And things started turning around. I still shot poorly, but I pulled down more boards than any other game in the series and had my highest plus-minus of the series at +17.

Ultimately, the main lesson you learn about criticism the

longer you do this is: The best way to respond is by putting in the work. In the UFC, Dana White always tells his fighters not to leave it up to the judges. He means end the fight with a KO. He means be so good that there is no debate about the winner. In the NBA, in any sport—heck, in life, really—you don't beat criticism by arguing with the critics. You beat it with your craft—by playing and winning. You don't prove doubters wrong with words, but with work.

Because at the end of the day, words are all they have—while you are the one putting your ass on the line, struggling, suffering, facing up to the possibility of failure every time you lace up your shoes. That's something the critic will never have.

The person who put this best was probably Teddy Roosevelt. His words about dealing with critics are famous, for good reason:

> It is not the critic who counts; not the man who points out how the strong man stumbles, or where the doer of deeds could have done them better. The credit belongs to the man who is actually in the arena, whose face is marred by dust and sweat and blood; who strives valiantly; who errs, who comes short again and again, because there is no effort without error and shortcoming; but who does actually strive to do the deeds; who knows great enthusiasms, the great devotions; who spends himself in a worthy cause; who at the best knows in the end the

triumph of high achievement, and who at the worst,
if he fails, at least fails while daring greatly, so that
his place shall never be with those cold and timid
souls who neither know victory nor defeat.

I can't top that, so I'll just leave with this: Criticism is easy. Putting in the work is hard. *Anything* you do to get better at your craft—one extra rep, one extra practice shot, one extra hour of film—is more important and more significant than a thousand pieces of criticism.

## LETTER 10

---

# THE NAME ON THE FRONT OF THE JERSEY IS WHAT COUNTS

Early on in my career, I heard a saying that's stuck with me. It's simple but profound: Play for the name on the front of the jersey, and they'll remember the name on the back.

It's hard to believe, but my career is living proof. In fact, there was a moment a few years ago that proved it.

It was March 26, 2019. I was walking through the tunnel at American Airlines Arena as I had done hundreds of times before. The crowd was thunderous, in a way I had never heard before. Or maybe I had just never listened like I was tonight—I was so eager to soak in every moment of it.

I had walked onto that same court for some big games. I had won my share of big games in front of that crowd. I had seen them in the streets of Miami as we celebrated our championships and I raised up the Larry O'Brien Trophy for them all to see.

But this was different.

Because I wasn't dressed to play. My jersey wasn't on me at all . . . instead, it was oversized and about to be lifted up to the rafters. The Miami Heat were retiring my number. This is an honor few athletes ever get, and only if many things go right and after many years of hard work.

Of all the players who have had their numbers retired across professional sports, the overwhelming majority were known for their individual accomplishments. Go to any arena or stadium in the country, look up at the numbers around the upper bowl, and ask that team's fans about the players those numbers represent. You'll hear things like, "He was a killer," or "She was unstoppable," or "He'd score thirty-five a night today, no doubt." You probably won't hear "He made everyone around him better" or "He was the glue that held everything together." Even if those things were true.

What was unusual about this moment for me was what Heat president and Hall of Famer Pat Riley chose to highlight from my career. He spoke not of the shots that I hit or the points I put on the board. He took the time to memorialize the final seconds of Game 6 in the 2013 NBA Finals. As Pat pointed out, it was Ray Allen who hit the last-second shot that tied the game and saved the series that we went on to win. But seconds before Ray hit that shot, I was the one who pulled down the rebound and got him the ball. Pat called it "the biggest assist in the history of the franchise."

It is hard to be great at the game, and for that reason, very rare. It is actually easier but strangely more rare to be a great teammate. When I got to Miami in 2010 to form the Big Three with LeBron and D-Wade, it could have gone bad very quickly. LeBron was in his ascendancy, but Miami was still D-Wade's town. Both guys like to have the ball in their hands. I myself was coming off seven straight seasons as the primary scorer up in Toronto, where I was, if I may humbly say so, a double-double machine. How was this going to work? Someone was going to have to get back and anchor the defense on one end and make sure the offense didn't bog down on the other end, while LeBron and D-Wade figured out how to play together within the context of our scheme. That was my job. I was the third leg of the stool. Some people called me a "role player" on the team, but that's not right. LeBron was a role player. D-Wade was a role player. Everyone on a winning team has a role to play. Winning takes everyone being on the same page about what the roles are.

It took a painful loss in the Finals, but we got there. When we got there we were humbled by losing—but we were hardened, too. And it showed. We were all willing to do the one extra little thing, whatever it was, to be there for our teammates, to transform from a collection of talented players into a true champion.

It may sound a bit quaint now that most NBA contenders are "superteams" of one kind or another, but that Heat team was really an experiment playing out in real time. And part of what made it work was that, aside from our Big Three, it was a team full of veteran guys who had your back, who wanted nothing more than to play winning basketball and take home rings. Even as I was finding my way, finding out who I was going to be in this new situation, figuring out how to be the third leg of the stool, I was learning from those guys. If anything helped me go from being The Man in Toronto to playing a different role in Miami, that was it.

Which is why it was even more special to me on this night in Miami to be honored for the kind of teammate I had been. I hope my kids, who were sitting on my lap as Pat Riley spoke, took that in. I hope the current Miami Heat roster and every other player watching did, too.

They were going to remember me forever in Miami not because I had put up the best numbers. Not because I had meticulously built my personal brand. Not because I had fought for my playing time harder than anyone else. No, they were doing it because I fought for the team.

I couldn't be prouder to be remembered for anything else.

Pat Riley got that, of course. It's something he has in common with all of the great coaches. Great coaches don't just teach fundamentals or draw up plays. They inspire a group of skilled athletes—never the type of people to have small egos—to put their egos on hold and come together for a greater purpose. Phil Jackson got it: "The strength of the team is each individual member," he said. "The strength of each member is the team." The Lakers even have a version of that in their facility. It's a quote from Kipling: "For the strength of the pack is the wolf, and the strength of the wolf is the pack." Coach K got it, too: "To me," he said, "teamwork is the beauty of our sport, where you have five acting as one."

That's what a team is all about: submerging your own ego in something greater than yourself. I think of the way Shane Battier spread the floor so LeBron could have more space to operate, or the way he took his turn defending the other team's best guy so LeBron could get a bit of a breather on the other end. Those are the kinds of sacrifices that build trust. I think of what Jeff Van Gundy said: "Don't fail the plan. Let the plan fail you." In other words, if the plan doesn't work, your coaches and teammates can fix it, as long as everyone is on the same page. But what can't be fixed is a group of guys who don't trust one another.

And when you've been lucky enough to have coaches and mentors who hammer that point into you—as I was—you start to see the beauty of the game in a way a more selfish athlete might not. I'll tell you about one of those times.

NBA Finals, 2013, Game 7 against the San Antonio Spurs. We won that game. Nobody probably remembers this except me, but, as I mentioned earlier, I didn't score a single point. We won. But I didn't score. Not once.

That game was such a lesson for me. Like most little kids with a ball, I used to imagine myself putting my team on my back in Game 7 of the Finals and carrying it to victory—and hitting the winning shot, too, for good measure. Imagining that shot is something that literally every basketball player, at every level, has in common. We've all done it. Even *Space Jam* starts with a scene of young Michael Jordan hitting a game-winning shot in his driveway. It's universal.

But in this real-life Game 7, my shots weren't falling. I was in foul trouble early—two fouls in the first half, and I had to sit. As I went to the bench, I couldn't help contrasting my fantasy Game 7s with how this real one was playing out. But before I could get too discouraged, I heard my old coach Sam Mitchell's voice in my head: "So what if you don't have any points? You can still get your teammates involved. You can still play hard on defense. You can still lead by example." The game has so many facets. There are so many different ways to shine in it. But whichever way is yours, you have to remember to approach it with 100 percent of your enthusiasm, 100 percent of your hustle. That's what being a good teammate requires. And when you win, whether you led the team in points or you came off the bench, you get to share the spotlight.

When I was back in the game, I had to D up Tim Duncan again. And when I could have been bitching and complaining about fouls, or getting too discouraged to give my all on the defensive end, I knew that winning came first. I'm proud of the defense I played on Duncan, especially with early foul trouble, which usually makes most guys play more tentative and the guys they're guarding get more aggressive. And while I didn't get to live out my fantasy Game 7, I got the satisfaction of knowing I could do whatever it took to help my teammates to victory.

When I got to hold that championship trophy, it didn't matter if I scored zero points or 50.

Fortunately, I'd had some experience with this kind of sacrifice, because the same thing happened in the Olympics five years earlier. I was chosen for the 2008 "Redeem Team"—the U.S. Olympic team that was supposed to redeem the disappointment of 2004, when the United States only won the bronze. It was amazing to represent my country. This was also the most talented team I'd ever been a part of. A team with Kobe, LeBron, Wade, and Carmelo—of course I was going to spend some time on the bench. I made the most of the minutes I got, I supported my teammates, and we took home the gold medal. I got to play out the closing minutes of a gold-medal game, something I'd dreamed about ever since watching the original Dream Team win the gold in 1992.

When every player comes with that attitude, you know your team is something special. On the other hand, teams are in for trouble when players aren't comfortable with their roles. I remember playing with one guy who just refused to accept his role that would've helped the team. He needed to set screens and rebound; instead he debated reasons he should get the ball more. He would always try to convince us that he had "game." Well, sure, it's the NBA—everyone's got game. But he was making it clear that he wasn't going to do everything it took to support his teammates. You can score? Great. But right now, this team needs you to pick, roll, and rebound. It made me think: Is this just about the money, like scorers get higher salaries? Maybe, but even if that's what motivates you, nothing gets you paid like being part of a winning team.

It was a little thing, but little things add up and poison successful organizations. How many championships did Kobe and Shaq leave on the table because they couldn't play together anymore? How about LeBron and Kyrie? Kyrie had a phenomenal series in the NBA Finals against the Warriors, hit the game-winning shot in Game 7, but at the end of the day he wanted to get out of LeBron's shadow. He wanted his own team. He wanted to be The Man.

You don't get to see the little things that build teams when you're watching a game on TV. All of those little things happen in the background. They're things like hosting a team dinner, or picking up your teammate after he misses a free throw, or cheering your team on from the bench. Sometimes a team needs your points—and sometimes it needs you to keep your head up when you're not getting the minutes you think you deserve. Those things add up—to a group of athletes who are truly willing to sacrifice for one another. The next time you watch an athlete take a brutal hit to clear space for his teammate, or you hear about Tim Duncan taking less money to clear up cap room for Popovich to grab him more talent, remember all of the little moments of team building that make those sacrifices possible.

Another way of saying that someone is a good teammate is just saying that they're trustworthy. You can trust them to be where the play says they're supposed to be, not off freelancing. You can trust them to have your back if a fight breaks out. You can trust them to sacrifice their stats to help the team win. You can trust them to give you constructive criticism on your game—not to put you down, but to build your game up. And that's what all the practices and midweek games in the middle of the regular season are all about— they're about teammates building trust in one another, learning to count on one another without stopping to think about it.

And trust, as they say, is a two-way street. You get it by giving it. When I pulled down that rebound in the Finals, I knew where Ray Allen was going to be, and I *knew* that he was going to hit that shot. And *he* knew that if he was where he was supposed to be, I was getting him the ball. It takes all 82 games in a season, and countless practices, to build that level of trust. When Ray joined our team on our second championship run, I remember thinking how important it was to get him comfortable fitting into our rotation during the regular season. He was making a transition like the one I made—from being The Man to changing roles and figuring it out on the fly. So I knew that that was one of my jobs—helping Ray get his shots, pulling down rebounds and looking for him at the top of the arc. We built the kind of trust that pays off in the biggest moments—moments like the last seconds of a game in the Finals.

Of course, I didn't figure out how to be a good teammate on my own. I did it by watching my teammates, guys who played the game beside me at all levels. When I was thinking about how

I could build trust with those guys on the Heat, I was thinking about what my own teammates taught me.

I was thinking about guys like José Calderón, who I played with on the Raptors. He was a guy who played the game with what I'd call purity. He was a pure point guard, always looking to get his teammates involved, always looking to pass first, always positive no matter what, always passionate about the game. He got better every year he played. When he came over from Spain, people used to say he wasn't an NBA player, but look at his career: thirteen years in the NBA, a FIBA World Cup, two silver Olympic medals and a bronze.

I was thinking of my guy Darrick Martin, who showed me how to be a veteran leader on the bench. Even though he didn't play that much, he understood what he was coming in for—to give the team energy and leadership in a tight spot. And he really took me under his wing and showed me how to work, what to expect. He never let me slide. He never let me take it easy. And he knew what it took for a person like me to fully mature into a player in the league.

Then there was my man Michael Curry. I only played with him for one year, but he was my vet. I remember his message for me from day one: "You've got a chance to be a really good player in this league, but you have got to put in the work. Here's what you do . . ."

And he showed me. He was there every day before practice, getting extra shots up, pushing me to put the extra work in—

even when I didn't feel like it. That's another huge part about being there for your teammates: being consistent, letting them trust that you're going to be there to put in the work every day, letting them know that you're going to be communicating consistently, leading consistently if you're a veteran leader, listening consistently if you're a young guy.

I looked up to Michael, because at the start of my career I still felt like a kid, and here was this grown man with a family and a whole career behind him, taking me under his wing. And besides that, he kept me out of trouble. I remember our first road trip in Miami. You can probably guess that I was getting ready to hit the clubs as soon as I could—not that I was going to go crazy or anything, but you know, it was Miami on a road trip, right? Well, as soon as we were done and in our street clothes, he grabbed me right away—"Let's go, young fella. Let's go out to eat. You're coming with me."

That's being a good teammate, too. I might've gotten into some shenanigans that night. And who knows—it might have derailed my path to being a great player in the league. Michael helped keep me on the path.

And there was my man Shane Battier. Everyone knows that Shane was one of the ultimate "glue guys." He was a tremendous teammate, and he was selfless. He wanted to win as much as anyone who ever played the game. That's all he cared about—win, win, win.

One time I asked Shane why he was always such a great

teammate—it's a weird question to ask—but he told me it was something he learned early, as early as first grade. He was a poor mixed-race kid in the suburbs of Detroit. He went to school with all white kids, and his dad was black, so he's the only person of color in the whole school—and he's tall. He was different. Mixed, tall, and poor.

He never fit in—which is what every kid wants when they're young. But he found that basketball was a way to do it. He used the term "social survival." And he understood that during recess or whenever everyone was playing—whether it was kickball, basketball, any sport—when his team won, people accepted him. He found out quickly that being there for his teammates could make him feel like he belonged.

And I saw it up close. He did whatever it took to help his team win. In Miami, that meant getting in a bar fight down low with bigger guys every night, guys with construction-worker muscle and old-man game like Zach Randolph and Kevin Garnett. He took those hits and came back every night for more, because that was part of the system our coach, Erik Spoelstra, wanted to implement. It meant playing "small ball," with smaller, faster guys at every spot on the floor. Shane got it, and he did what it took. He said that his strategy in the pros was to make it impossible for a coach to live without him. There's a reason he was a champion at every level: not just his talent, but his intelligence and his drive. Every team needs a Shane Battier.

And then, of course, there's D-Wade. What I respect so much

about him, besides his talent, is how much extra work he put in behind the scenes to make the Big Three in Miami work. You didn't see it on the court, but getting us all to jell took a lot of dinners, a lot of private conversations, a lot of work trying to figure out how we were each going to play a new role. D-Wade led that. And, like I said, Miami was his town—and that meant he took the lead in making his new teammates feel at home.

It wasn't just talking basketball. You know, after a while, you get tired of talking X's and O's, and someone says, "Hey, man, what else is going on in your life?" You know what Dwyane was capable of on the court, but you should see him off the court. He's a true leader—the kind of guy who is always going to push you to be your best, and also the kind of guy you can come to to talk about anything in your life.

But, you know, something funny happens when you play in the league for as long as I did. You look around, and one day, you realize that the younger guys are looking to you for guidance. One day, without exactly realizing when it happened, you're some young guy's role model. And when I got to that point in my career, I was so lucky that I could look back on all of those great teammates in my past and draw on their examples.

If the young guys watching me could learn something from how I played and practiced, I hope they learned that basketball is a business. That phrase gets thrown around a lot whenever people get traded—it tells them to be unsentimental and unattached, because your team's GM may not be attached to you. But that's not what I mean by it. I mean that we're doing a job—we have to show up to work every day, and we can't waste a single one. I know how tempting it is to take a day off—in practice, or even in the middle of a game in the regular season—to give up a bit and say, "Well, it's just one lost day."

But this is a business—it's our work, our calling. And if we're taking a day off, I guarantee you that the competition isn't. So I always tried to take the young guys under my wing—like the way the vets took me under their wing—and push them. I did it because I wanted us to win. But I also did it because I genuinely cared about their success, and I know how much having an older guy care about your success can make a difference when you're just starting out.

I remember how one of my teammates told me, "I just want to see you do well." That stuck with me—and I tried to let my younger teammates know that I wanted the same thing for them. That's what a teammate is: someone who wants every single person on the team, not just himself, to do well.

Contrast that maybe with that perennial struggle between the aging quarterback and the new draft pick. "I'm not here to mentor," they famously say. You gotta fight for your spot on your own.

I'm not here to judge that mentality. Because I get that there is more behind it than just self-interest. For me, it was harder to groom younger players than it might have been for some veterans. Not because I was selfish—though who doesn't worry about being replaced?—but because I'm a quiet guy by nature, and breaking out of my shell was hard work. I still wish I could've been a bit more talkative, made a few more connections, gone to a few more team dinners, reached out to a few more guys who needed something I could teach them. But I did work to come out of that shell, and I'm proud of that.

So, just as I have my own list of guys—the teammates who inspired me to become who I am today—I hope I'm on someone else's list of guys. I hope I passed along some of the knowledge that others passed on to me: knowledge not just about the tricks of our trade, but about how to be a man. They say the human brain doesn't stop developing until about age twenty-five, right? Well, most of the guys who come into the league are a good bit younger than that. They're still works in progress—both as professional athletes and as men. And I hope I did for them a bit of what my veteran teammates did for me.

Most of all, I wanted them to trust me—because, like I said, there's no teamwork without trust. I never wanted to be flashy. Just solid and reliable and trustworthy. I never wanted my guys to doubt, even for a second, that I was going to have their backs, that I was going to step up to the moment without fear. No matter what, no matter how big the fight, I wanted them to know that they could rely on me to make the extra pass, to set the extra pick, to do whatever was necessary to win.

My jersey is going to be up in the rafters as long as the Miami Heat play basketball. But just as important to me, I hope that who I was as a teammate lives on in the young guys I played with, and I hope they pass it on when it's their turn.

Who knows where sports will take you. Maybe you'll get breaks that I did and find yourself a pro. Maybe you'll top out in high school or college. It doesn't matter. The one skill that will carry you forward in life, the best thing you can take from the game—whatever that game is for you—is the ability to be a teammate.

To be of use to others. To want others to do well . . . and to help yourself do well by helping them.

# WINNING AND LOSING: NOT TOO HIGH, NOT TOO LOW

know you probably don't read much poetry, but that's OK. Most poems are not my style anyway.

But there is one, "If" by Rudyard Kipling, which was written as a piece of advice to his son, that I've come to love, as a player and as a father. Essentially, it's a poem about all the things you have to be able to do—all the different kinds of mental strength you have to cultivate—before you can consider yourself a grown-up. It's a classic, and you should read the whole thing.

But I want to focus on just a couple of lines from it. They might sound like total anathema to your mindset as an athlete—which is exactly why I want to talk about them with you. It's good to be challenged on our most deeply held assumptions. It's good to get to the uncomfortable truth of things.

The verse is this:

*If you can meet with Triumph and Disaster*
*And treat those two impostors just the same*

He's talking about winning and losing. He's saying you can't let either one change you—*either one.*

There was a point in my life where I probably would have said that anyone who tried to say that there was no difference between winning and losing was just a *loser.* Losers make excuses about trying their best, about it all just being a game. Winners win. Right?

*Winning isn't everything, it's the only thing.* Right?

But over the years, I've won enough and lost enough to have some perspective on this. I hope I have the credibility to talk to you about it. So let me explain what I mean and how there's a great deal of wisdom in the approach to life he's talking about. If you can understand it, it'll make you happier—and, though this is a bit of a paradox, it may help you win more and lose less.

When I first got into the league, it was tough handling losing. Wins were few and far between. But there was something a teammate told me, and it always stuck with me: "Don't get too high, don't get too low. Stay in the middle."

Playing so many games in the league, you have to learn how to continue your life, both on and off the court, regardless of any game's outcome. You have to handle *both* losing and winning. You have to keep them from bringing you too far down or pumping you up too much. So what if you blew a 15-point lead on your home court with seven minutes left? It's embarrassing, sure. But you'd better get over it, because you'll be out there again in a day or two.

"Don't get too high, don't get too low." That's the mentality that keeps a single loss from turning into a devastating losing streak, and that keeps a big win from turning into destructive overconfidence.

I've talked quite a bit about winning my rings with the Heat. I've talked about those two championships because they are, no question, among the greatest moments of my life. I'm sure you've seen videos of a team, whichever team, popping champagne and celebrating in the locker room after a championship. Well, I've been there, a couple of times, and I can tell you that the videos barely capture it. It's the feeling of having a dream for years, and then watching it materialize in front of you, in real time. In sports, when that clock hits zero, you know who won and who lost. And if you won it all, that's a feeling nothing and no one can take away from you. It's about the highest high you can get.

But let me tell you about a loss. In March 2003, Georgia Tech lost to Texas Tech in the quarterfinals of the NIT. That was my last game as a college basketball player. Sure, the whole thing was a bit anticlimactic—I mean, we weren't even in the NCAA tournament. We barely had a winning record that year, and it was pretty clear that we weren't going to go on a run and end up cutting down the nets at the Final Four. I was pretty sure that I was going pro at that point, so I was almost positive that it was my last game as soon as the horn sounded at the end of the fourth quarter. I know, I had the pros to look forward to—and as I explained earlier, college ball was hard for me in a lot of ways. But no matter what, it was the end of a chapter of my life.

It was the kind of loss that is literally impossible to do over. I knew not only that I wouldn't be cutting down the nets at the end of that season, but that I'd *never* get to do that. Every kid who's ever dreamed of playing college hoops has watched the "One Shining Moment" montage at the end of the National Championship game that culminates with the winning team's players in hats and T-shirts, each holding a piece of the net that they climbed up the ladder and cut down themselves. I'd be lying to you if I said not getting to do that, or even have a shot at it, only hurt a little.

A major win and a major loss. Do you know what I did after both these things? I did the thing that true pros do after any game, regardless of the outcome: I got back to work. I watched film. I asked for feedback from my coaches. I turned my mind toward the next game—even if the next game was in a new season, or at a new level of the sport. How do you erase a loss? By winning again. How do you show a big win was not a fluke? By winning again.

You want to celebrate a big win? Go ahead. I love celebrating wins. Who doesn't enjoy a parade? Especially when *it's in your honor*. But just remember, you have a big X on your back now, and while you're celebrating, other people are preparing.

You want to hang your head after a big loss? Go ahead. You don't have to ask me—I *know* how much losing hurts. But every day you spend feeling sorry for yourself is a day you lose to work on erasing the pain of that loss in the only way that will last.

None of that is to downplay the pain of losing. You play the game, you're gonna lose. Whatever the game is. Everyone has losses in life—your top school rejects you, you ask someone out on a date and get turned down—but athletes feel those losses in a dramatic way, because losing in sports is undeniable (there's no spinning a loss as a win) and because it happens in front of an audience. There's a reason you see college players sobbing on the bench when they get eliminated from March Madness, or kids collapsing on the field when they're out of the Little League World Series. There's no way of talking yourself out of what just happened. You lost. Pros might not break down and cry as often, but that's not necessarily because we're tougher. It's because by the time you've gotten to the pros, you've lost *a lot* in your life. We might not break down, but it still hurts.

Of course, a huge loss is the flip side of every huge win.

One of the most epic shots in recent years was Kawhi Leonard's Game 7 game-winner against the Sixers in the 2019 playoffs. You can probably picture it—a deep shot from the corner over Joel Embiid that touched every part of the rim before dropping in. It bounced around for so long up there that Kawhi had time to crouch down behind the baseline and watch it fall. Of the million shots I've watched in the league, in person or on TV, I can probably count on one hand the number of shots as crazy as that one. And at the buzzer? *In Game 7?* Damn.

But think about it from the perspective of the other team. The Sixers weren't favored in that series, but they played the eventual champions to a draw right up to literally the last second. They played good defense on the last play, too—if you can force your opponent into a shot like the one Kawhi had to take, that's a solid defensive possession. The Sixers did everything they were supposed to do—and it wasn't enough.

I've been there. It feels surreal. *We were great out there—did we just lose?* To top it off, the camera caught Embiid crying right after the buzzer. I've been there, too—one of the rawest, most emotional moments in your life, and it's on national TV.

And you have to lace up next season and bounce back. Which is what he did. And what you have to do.

I remember something a well-known musician told me once: "If I go into the studio and record a great album, that's a win for me. But I don't do it in real time, with everyone watching. When you guys win, you win in front of everybody. That's amazing." And yeah, it is. But when we lose, we lose in front of everybody, too. Pretty much any night of the season when there is a full slate of games, you can turn on your TV and watch more than a hundred athletes in the prime of their lives, and at the peak of their powers, getting their asses beat and having to process that fact right in front of you, in real time.

I know what that's like, because I've been on the bad end of that equation. When we were upset in the 2011 Finals by the Dallas Mavericks, their stars—Dirk Nowitzki, Jason Kidd, Jason Terry—had been to the Finals before, and they'd lost. In case they needed any extra motivation, they lost to the Heat the last time they were in the Finals, and they were out to avenge that loss.

They understood, on a deeper level than we did, that they might not ever get back to the Finals, and so they played with a different sense of urgency. They dove for those 50-50 balls—the loose balls on the floor, the contested rebounds—a little harder than we did. And over the course of a series, that matters— turning those 50-50 tossups into 51-49 in your favor. They knew the pain of losing, and they played like they never wanted to feel that pain again. It was a big part of why they won.

On the other hand, our minds just weren't cultivated enough to handle the pressure. When we won the first game, I remember feeling cocky, like we'd wrapped up the series already. When we lost the second game, I remember a tremendous letdown, like we'd blown the whole thing already. Our highs were too high, and our lows were too low. That determined steadiness a team needs to just shut down and dominate any opposition? We didn't have it. And over the course of a whole series, against an oppo- nent with more maturity and mental stability than we had, it made a big difference. Looking back on that Dallas series, I think resiliency was our weakness, mentally and physically.

I remember how losing that series took me right back to being a ten-year-old again. As we were walking off the court, I think somebody said, "Better luck next year." I don't know why, but that almost made me lose it right there. I thought of all the hard work we'd put in, all the people who had doubted us, how long the season was—and it was just crushing. You spend your whole life dreaming of getting to the Finals, but you never once imagine making it all the way there and then blowing it. That's what it felt like to us. I would have done anything to make that pain go away. Then, to make matters worse, I cried on national TV! I was so embarrassed. I wanted to crawl into a hole.

And that motivation was a big part of why *we* won it all the next year.

The pain of losing like that is like rocket fuel. If you mishandle it, it can blow up—and destroy you. But if you protect it, channel it, and ignite it at just the right time—watch out.

If you handle it right, nothing motivates you like losing. The more it hurts, the better. Because you can remember that feeling. And because you'd do anything not to feel like that again, right? So you work harder, you put in the extra reps, you show up to the gym an hour earlier. That was my feeling after every loss when I was young—not just the pain of losing, but the second-guessing of all the extra work I could've put in. So I realized that if I couldn't control the pain of losing—sometimes you lose no matter how much you deserve to win—I could at least control the pain of second-guessing my own effort. *Man, these sprints hurt.* Do they hurt more than losing? No? Then get back out there.

I think one of the most infamous basketball losses in recent years came in the 2018 NCAA tournament. You probably remember it: UVA was the first No. 1 seed *ever* to lose to a No. 16 seed. And they didn't just lose. They got their asses kicked. They lost by *20*. True, they lost their best player to injury just days before, but it shouldn't have been enough to lose, and definitely not to lose by that much. Imagine the humiliation of knowing you'll be the answer to that trivia question for the rest of history. But you probably also know what happened next: UVA came back and won the whole damn thing the next year.

I can't put it any better than their coach, Tony Bennett, who was on the sidelines for the loss and for the win: "All the ridicule, all the criticism, all the humility, all the things that happened, at that moment, it was crystal clear that it was all worth it. . . . If you learn to use it right, the adversity, it will buy you a ticket to a place you couldn't have gone any other way."

I know what he's talking about, because I've earned a lot of those tickets and I have bought a few. You can't have a long career in basketball and not earn them over time. Among American pro sports leagues, basketball (along with hockey) is second only to baseball in the number of games in a season—82 games a year. Plus the playoffs! I played for thirteen seasons as a pro. I played in a total of 982 games. I lost *437 games*, including 32 in the playoffs. I can't even calculate how many times I lost over the course of my career in total, if you include AAU, high school, college, the pros, and the national team. I wouldn't say I'm *comfortable* with losing, but I'm well acquainted.

You have to be if you're an athlete. Or if you want to do anything big.

Losing is still your enemy, but you learn how to live with it once you put the swords away. Peyton Manning has one of the highest completion percentages of all time. But it's only 65.3 percent. He threw 251 interceptions. Some of those interceptions cost his team the game—in a few heartbreaking situations, it ended their season.

And, of course, there's this famous fact about how hard it is to hit a baseball. If you bat .400 in the major leagues, you're a Hall of Famer. The last guy to do that was Ted Williams—almost *eighty* years ago. But even if you have that kind of insane success, it still means that you're failing to get a hit six out of ten times. Even Ted Williams failed at the plate more often than he succeeded.

Mark Zuckerberg is worth billions of dollars, but he's also the CEO who on July 26, 2018, oversaw the single largest drop in market cap for a company in history—$120 billion in one day. Oof. He's the CEO who successfully bought Instagram on the cheap, one of the greatest acquisitions in modern business, but also failed in his multiple attempts to buy Snapchat. There is no country, no general, no leader, no team with a perfect record. None.

You want to be a great? Get ready to lose—painfully, undeniably, in front of an audience—more than pretty much anyone in any other calling.

I don't know how hard learning that lesson is for most athletes, or how hard it will be for you, but I'll tell you it was really hard for me because I *hate* losing. Growing up, I was always a sore loser. It took me years and years to be able to handle losing, to be mature enough to lose well. When I was a kid, I'd cry after every loss. My dad thought there was something wrong with me—true story. When I was a teenager, I didn't cry about it anymore—I just got pissed.

One of those losses really sticks with me: We were 32–2, we were in the running for the state championship, and we lost in the final four to Lanier High School out of San Antonio—a team that, to be honest, we totally underestimated. The funny thing was, Lanier had lost in the finals the year before. And part of the reason they wanted it so much more than we did was because they knew what losing felt like. We didn't know what it felt like, and once we did, we didn't know why it hurt the way it did. Or at least I didn't. Part of it was embarrassment—knowing that my classmates and my friends and my family saw me come up short. Part of it was shame. Whatever it was, losing has never stopped hurting.

As I grew up, I learned that accepting losing doesn't make you a loser—it makes you brave. You have to put everything you have out there on the line and know that it might still not be enough. The more losing hurts, the more you have to risk. As I figured that out, I was learning that losing and coming back the next day takes real, serious, grown-up courage.

Some people have defense mechanisms around losing. You know, stuff like, "Oh, it's not that important. It's all good. I'm fine." Plenty of people make excuses after a loss—it was bad luck, or it was the refs, or their coach had a better game plan. Whatever. Lots of people point fingers at anyone but themselves when they lose. I know—I've done it more than I'm proud to admit. I've seen teammates blame teammates, or the coach, or the altitude, or lack of sleep, or the refs. I've done that myself, too. All of those excuses are ways of dodging the truth of what really happened. It takes strength to face the truth: You lost because you lost. Most of the time, you just got outplayed. Live with that, and figure out how to come back better next time. But whenever you point the finger at someone other than yourself, you're losing a precious opportunity to get better.

That's true *even if* you did get hosed by a bad call. If you focus on the bad call, you're throwing away the motivational fuel that will get you through the next practice, or the next season. You can't choose whether or not the refs blow a huge call. But you can choose where to put your mental energy.

When you lose, it takes real courage to say, "You know what? It's not all good. It sucks." You have to take that pain and turn it inward—into motivation to be better next time. Then you have to suit up for the next one, and play your heart out without fear of how much it's going to hurt if you lose again.

You figure out how to learn from those losses. You learn how to benefit from them. You learn how—and this is an important balance—to do it gracefully, while never resigning yourself to it. Anyone can lose, but it takes real mental strength to *lose well.*

How do you do it? Well, experience helps. But it's also learning that you're the same person whether you win or lose—that you can take pride in how you play regardless of what the scoreboard says. That's not the same as saying, "It's all good. It's just a game." It means recognizing that there are important things about playing the game that don't end up in the final result. And beyond that, it just matters that you're in the arena—and you can take pride in that, too. You're out there taking the risk of losing, putting all you have on the line, and most people in the stands can't say that. There's honor in playing your heart out, whatever the result.

And when you do win, it feels that much better. How can winning feel special if you don't know what losing feels like? There's no hot without cold, there's no light without dark, right? Well, there's no winning without losing. And winning, for very frustrating reasons, is actually harder to handle than losing. The consequences are much more insidious.

I've been at the pinnacle of my sport four times, in 2011, 2012, 2013, and 2014. Fifty percent of the time we lost. Fifty percent of the time we won. In those two middle years, we took home the crown. Yet even though the two championship results were the same on the outside, the two times I got to hold the championship trophy felt entirely different.

In 2012, the feeling was more like relief. We'd exorcised the demons of our upset loss the year before. We'd silenced the doubters who said our team was too me-first, too ego-driven to succeed at the highest level. And I'd shut up my own internal critic—the one who comes after you at the end of a bad game, or when you're in the middle of a shooting slump, telling you that you'll never make it to the top. Winning in 2012 was proof that all of the doubters, inside and outside, were wrong.

But right from the beginning, our goal wasn't just *one* championship. It was *multiple* championships. So I took some time to enjoy the win that summer—and then I got back to the gym.

Our whole team knew that each year was going to get harder, not just because we were all a year older and potentially a year more complacent, but because every team in the league had another year's worth of scouting and intel on us. Now that you're the champs, people expect more things from you, hate you a little more. Underdogs and young challengers can sneak up on everyone, but once you've won it all, you're under the microscope until you lose. If you think people are going to respect you just because you won a championship—you're wrong. If you think people are going to bow down to you or roll over for you—you're wrong. Everyone is gunning for you. Everyone wants to knock you off. Naysayers and doubters come out of the woodwork, all with a reason why your win was a fluke, or why anyone can get lucky once, or why you don't stack up to the greats of the past.

It's like running on a treadmill—to win the next year, you have to be even better, you have to run faster just to stay in place. At the same time, we had to adjust to new teammates, like Ray Allen—and learning how to play with new teammates at the highest level takes a season at least.

So, despite all that, when we won again in 2013, I think the feeling is best described as *elation*. I knew that our success wasn't some fluke. I knew that my teammates and I could keep our egos in check for two straight years. I knew what it felt like to choose to be a team player, and to watch that sacrifice for my teammates pay off. It's hard to describe, but in 2012, I felt like we *won*; in 2013, I felt like we were *winners*.

I remember crying after that game—a lot of guys did. I'd watch people win championships on TV and I always wondered, "Why the hell are you crying?" Well, I found out. It's like all of the emotions you have to keep a handle on—your self-doubt, your fear of being a fluke, your exhaustion—come pouring out of your body.

It's an amazing feeling. But it's also a dangerous place to be. As you know, and as I think about all the time, we never got back there as a team. The next time, the Spurs took us in five games.

John Wooden said, "Winning takes talent. To repeat takes character." To win repeatedly, you have to push through adversity even when the hunger you experienced when you were just a young challenger to the throne is sated. You can't be driven by a need to prove yourself, because you've already proven yourself. You have to be driven by a love of excellence, by a desire to play the game at the highest possible level for as long as you possibly can. And every time you succeed, some of your external motivation gets chipped away, until all you have left is that inner commitment to excellence. When Pat Riley took the stage at the Lakers' championship parade in 1987 and said, "We're gonna win it again"—guaranteeing a repeat victory before the team had even finished celebrating the first one—it sounded crazy, or just plain arrogant. But Riley knew his team, and he knew they could rise to the challenge. He definitely didn't win a popularity contest by saying that while his team was thinking about their summer vacations. The next year, that Lakers team became the first to win back-to-back championships in almost two decades.

Basketball, like most sports, is rigged to make success harder for a winning team every year. The defending champions get the lowest draft pick. They played more games the previous season than every team but the runner-up. Their top players often leave to chase money and individual success elsewhere; assistant coaches get poached for head coaching jobs elsewhere. And, on the level of intangibles, winning can be a great demotivator. All of this makes sustained success the true test of character. And in this way, basketball can be a lot like the rest of life. It's not that hard to be young and hungry. It's much harder to be older, and successful, and *still* hungry.

Think of the great dynasties: Jordan's Bulls, the early-'90s Cowboys, the late-'90s Yankees. You might hate them—plenty of people do. But you've got to *respect* them. Teams like that don't just string together several championships in a row. They're effectively playing the game on a harder setting, year after year. That's what makes sustained success so awe-inspiring. Those teams stayed committed to excellence even as all of the external motivation for winning was getting chipped away year after year.

Watch a guy like Steph Curry hit shot after shot in warmups—after he has absolutely nothing left to prove in the game of basketball—and you get an intuitive sense of what it means to treat winning and losing like impostors. It's not that winning stops feeling great, or that losing stops hurting. It's that he warms up the same, and plays with the same heart, whether or not he won or lost the night before. He controls what he can control, and lets the rest go. He takes pride in the beautiful things in the game—the swish of a jumper, a crisp pass to a cutting teammate—that are beautiful whether you're up 20 or down 20.

And because a player like that understands that the game is bigger than him, he never lets a win get him too high, and he never lets a loss get him too low. Seneca, one of the great Stoic philosophers, understood that idea way before there was a game called basketball. About two thousand years ago, he wrote down some advice about how fathers can help their sons learn to be good sports:

> In contests with his comrades we ought not to allow
> him to become sulky or fly into a passion: let us see
> that he be on friendly terms with those whom he
> contends with, so that in the struggle itself he may
> learn to wish not to hurt his antagonist but to con-
> quer him: Whenever he has gained the day or done
> something praiseworthy, we should allow him to en-
> joy his victory, but not to rush into transports of de-

light: for joy leads to exultation, and exultation leads
to swaggering and excessive self-esteem.

The point is that being a good sport is good *for you*, not just
for the people you're competing against. Sulking when you lose
and acting like a jackass when you win both make it harder for
you to get better. In different ways, both destroy your excellence.

That's why even the biggest winners have to keep winning in
perspective. In 2001, I was a high school All-American, and
Kobe Bryant came to talk to us at a training camp. This was in
the middle of his great run with Shaq on the Lakers. I remember
him saying something like, "If you think winning is going to
complete you, you're wrong." He told us that there's always going
to be a next season, there's going to be another champion next
year, and even if you repeat, one year you won't. The high of
winning is temporary, and if you make chasing that high into
your identity, it's going to let you down. That's always stuck with
me—as tempting as it is to do it, I've never treated winning as
something that will complete me as a person. Of course, those
words seem even more meaningful to me now that Kobe is gone.

Winning and losing are both impostors, and I say that to you
as someone who danced with both for four consecutive years. I'm
not being flip. When you have real mental strength, you know
that your worth and your deep-down happiness don't depend on
the scoreboard. Winning doesn't give you that peace of mind,
and losing doesn't have to take it away.

Now, one of the reasons we love sports is because they're an exaggeration of real life. In sports, the buzzer sounds and you know beyond a shadow of a doubt who won and who lost. There's a great quote from a novel by Sergio de la Pava, where he describes a football team owner giving a pep talk to her players before a big game: "The overwhelming majority of people devote their energies to endeavors that have no clear-cut winners or losers, no scores. Part of what that means is they can fool themselves if they have to. You won't have that luxury. . . . Every Sunday a score will be created and it will tell you your worth as a craftsman. At the end this team will have a record and it will tell you even more." The great NFL coach Bill Parcells put it more succinctly: "You are what your record says you are."

Life—life outside your sport, at least—is a lot messier than that. You can look back on something you thought at the time was a big win and realize that that's where it all started to go wrong. Or you can look back on what seemed to be a loss and realize that it put you on the right path. Or you can deceive other people, or yourself, into thinking a loss was really a win.

In every other part of your life other than your sport, you won't really have a record—at least not one that's as clear-cut as 16–0 or 8–8. You'll have a *life*. But if there's one thing you can take from sports into the rest of your life, it's that refusal to fool yourself. Don't fool yourself into treating a loss like a win. But more than that, don't fool yourself into thinking that winning—at school, at your job, at money, at your love life, whatever—will complete you. It won't. There are plenty of winners whom life later reveals to be real losers.

To me, that's why we have to be gracious, regardless of the outcome. I was struck, watching *The Last Dance*, with the contrast between the sight of Isiah Thomas and Bill Laimbeer not shaking hands with the Bulls after the '91 Eastern Conference Finals and the footage of Karl Malone chasing down the Bulls' bus after that last Finals, getting on it, and walking all the way to the back—past the guys who had just beaten him for the second year in a row—to get to Jordan to shake his hand. That is a man who has conquered himself, his emotions, his soul, I'll tell you that. Just the thought of that gives me chills the same way that some of the most impressive feats I've seen on the court do.

Like I wrote to you earlier, you need to find a *why* that can power you through wins and losses, with all of the dangers of each— a why that can keep you pushing on when you want to lie down and quit. That's what makes you impressive. Not your record. That's what gets you through a life that will be filled with more moments of triumph and disaster than you can anticipate.

# DO THE WORK. DO. THE. WORK.

How do you become a champion?

What does it take?

The only answer I know, that I like, comes from Trevor Moawad, the mental skills coach who works with Russell Wilson.

"It takes," he says, *"what it takes."*

Like a lot of wisdom that still resonates today, that idea has ancient roots. In Roman times, the Stoic philosopher Epictetus said essentially the same thing: "Athletes decide first what they want to be, then proceed to do what is necessary."

Do what is necessary. It takes what it takes.

It's that simple. It's that complicated. But it's possible.

You have to believe that if it's possible for someone to do it, then it is possible for *you* to do it. That's a really powerful idea. I grew up watching Magic and Jordan—maybe you grew up watching me, or maybe for you it was Steph and KD. Maybe you relate to Spud Webb, or maybe you relate to Shaquem Griffin or Thomas Hitzlsperger or Lisa Leslie. But whoever it is, the things these people have accomplished for their sport and for their causes, this was not done by a superhero. Jackie Robinson was not an alien. He was a *man*. He was a human being, like you and me, who was willing to put in the work to make the most of his talent, and to do what it takes. What the pioneers did was possible because it was humanly possible. That means it's possible for us, too.

You have no way of knowing ahead of time how much excellence is going to cost. It's not something with a price tag on it. But every single time it presents you with a new demand, you have to pay up. If you knew what it was going to cost before you started—"hit ten thousand free throws, run a thousand wind sprints, and do five hundred pull-ups and you'll be a champion"— anyone could do it. Or almost anyone. What's hard isn't just the work. What's hard is giving everything you have with no guarantees but the love of the game.

*It takes what it takes.*

*Every day.*

*Of your whole life.*

And even then, it might not be enough.

I know how much you want to be successful. I wanted it, too. I told myself I was ready to put in the work. I knew how hard my heroes had worked. I knew how many hours they spent in the gym, about guys who wouldn't leave practice before they hit a certain number of shots. I heard about how Tiger Woods was the only athlete at Stanford with his own key to the football program's weight room—even though he was on the golf team.

My heroes would always talk about the work they put in on their way to the top. The interviews of their old coaches from high school and Little League would talk about how hard they worked. There was always some legend about how much they were in the gym when they were a kid. I wanted to be like them. I wanted to emulate what they put into the game.

So I knew hard work was important. But when I started down this road, I didn't know what hard work *was*. No kid does. Not yet.

I had talent. That made me lucky. But it also made me unlucky in a way, because the game came so easily to me at first that I underestimated how much work greatness would take. Maybe the same thing has happened to you. But one day you find out that to get to that next level, to really be great, it's going to take more than you'd imagined.

That's what hard work means. Pushing your body and mind past their limits, again and again—with no promise that you're going to get where you want to go. *When you ain't nothing but tired*—we talked about that already. But it's more than pushing through fatigue. It's the long haul journey of the whole thing, the repetition of it, the dedication of one's life to a craft. If success were promised, the work wouldn't be nearly as hard. It takes what it takes.

*We're talking about practice?* Yeah. We are talking about practice. There are no games, no championships, no MVPs, no signing bonuses, no flawless behind-the-back passes or perfectly executed alley-oops, no comeback-from-behind wins without practice.

Nothing happens without hard work.

Do you want to accomplish your dreams, win trophies, make a million dollars, be a champion, be famous, whatever it is? Great. Everyone wants something like that. It doesn't even have to be that big. Do you want to write a book, play the piano, get straight As, learn another language? Great. Everyone wants something like that, too.

Or rather, they want to *have* those things.

Do they want to earn them?

Do they want to pay whatever it takes?

Nah.

Kobe Bryant once gave an interview about the training he'd put in when he was still a young kid. Every night, he'd go to bed and visualize himself getting hot in an NBA game, hitting shot after shot, until he'd get up to 120 points or some other ridiculous number.

Lots of young kids do that. Here's what made Kobe different: The next day, he'd go out and take the shots he visualized. He'd put up practice shots every day. And not just a bunch of random shots—but from every position on the court, in every possible scenario. Corner threes. Fadeaways from the post. Jumpers off a screen. No matter what happened in a real game, he wanted to be prepared for it, mentally and physically. "When you download that into your system," he said, "you go out on the court and you're just executing things that you've done thousands of times before."

Every coach I have ever had has some story like that, of the legendary practice habits of one great or another. I had an assistant coach who knew Steve Nash, and he told me that Steve and Dirk Nowitzki would go back to the court every night—whether they'd just played a game or not—and put up hundreds of shots. Every night, the both of them. And that was kind of their routine. After a while I thought, *Damn, if the best shooter in the world is doing that every night, I'd better be doing that, too.* In basketball, as in everything else, you get out what you put in.

And it turns out that for every player I idolized, there were stories about the tremendous amount they put into their game when the cameras were off and the other players had called it a day. I remember the first time I saw a skinny kid like me in the NBA. Shooting the outside jumper. Blocking shots. I loved it, because skinny post guys never got much love. In an instant I had a model I could follow in my own career. The skinny kid's name was Kevin Garnett. I didn't just watch KG play. I had posters of him on my bedroom wall. I consumed everything I could find about him, every article, every interview. Every time he dropped a clue about what he did to get to the top of the game, I followed it religiously.

One of my luckiest breaks starting out in the league was that one of my coaches, Sam Mitchell, who was a former pro, had also been KG's mentor. And it was my good fortune that Sam was full of KG stories. I'd always ask him, "How did KG work on his post game? How did he improve his jump shot?" Things like that. The specifics in Sam's stories varied by subject—you don't do the same thing to perfect a drop step in the low post as you do to come off a screen for a catch-and-shoot jumper—but the stories themselves shared a common thread: KG was in the gym every day, putting in the work.

I don't know who your hero is, but I can promise you: Whoever it is, they didn't get to that point by taking it easy. They worked at it more than you can imagine.

If you ever watch an athlete you admire and wonder how they can execute under pressure, it's because they've simulated that pressure in practice, over and over and over, until it became routine. Kobe hit so many clutch shots because, in part, he spent so much of his life imagining himself hitting clutch shots in practice. "I did it a million times as a kid," he said. "And I never failed, because I was the timekeeper. If I missed, I'd always put a second back on the clock."

I'll never forget the mechanics of the amazing shot that Ray Allen hit in the closing seconds of regulation in Game 6 of the 2013 Finals to save our team from defeat. When I pulled down the rebound in traffic, I found him leaking naturally back out to the corner. When I kicked it out to him, he caught the ball while instinctively stepping back behind the three-point line without paying any attention to where his feet were. Before I could even reset to crash the boards, Ray already had the ball in the pocket, had elevated, and was releasing the shot in one fluid motion, which all took less than a second to come together. After we won the series, Allen told a reporter, "I'd say I've taken that shot several hundreds of thousands of times." That *exact* shot.

And he'd taken pretty much every shot, from pretty much everywhere else on the court, thousands of times, too. He had a whole set list of shots he'd practice from every spot on the court, and would practice hitting every shot again and again, to the point of exhaustion, just to make sure he could hit them when his body was screaming at him at the end of the fourth quarter. Jumper after jumper. Drill after drill. Not just jumpers standing in place, but shots on the move, catch-and-release, coming off a screen, one dribble, two dribbles, pull-up jumpers, short jumpers, midrange jumpers, threes, face-up jumpers out of the post, fadeaways . . . Before every game, he'd start going through his set list of shots four hours before tip-off. He said he didn't want to shoot a shot for the first time that day during the game.

Here's the sneaky thing about practice that they don't tell you when you're coming up: The need for it *never* stops; it actually increases. That shot Ray hit to take the game to overtime? That was in his *seventeenth* year in the league, his first with us in Miami. He didn't start a single game for us. He barely played half of each game. But more than half of his shot attempts every game were three-pointers. Shots just like he hit with six seconds left and our championship hopes on the line. I've seen Ray practice—I'd be willing to bet he practiced those step-back corner threes more in Year 17 than he did in Year 7, and more in Year 7 than in Year 1. Because as Ray made his way in the league, his job became more and more focused on hitting those jumpers, which meant he had to be more and more focused on putting in that work.

These days, Steph Curry is the same way. He puts up three hundred extra shots *after* each practice. In 2017, ESPN reported that he and his teammates were hitting so many practice shots that they were literally destroying the nets in their practice facility. It's no surprise then that Steph and Ray are probably 1 and 2 in any ranking of the greatest shooters of all time. Many parents bring their kids to Golden State Warriors games early, to watch Stephen Curry go through his exhaustive (and exhausting) pre-game routine. Steph has nothing to prove. He's a unanimous league MVP, he's a multi-time All-Star, and he's a multi-time champion.

Yet, there he is every night, before every game, going through his two-handed dribble drills, working at getting just a little bit better at this skill or that move. Just think how easy it could be for him to maybe shave a couple of reps off each drill, or to reduce the number of total drills in the routine, or to retire his famous pre-game tunnel shot to close out his routine when the Warriors are at home. No one could blame him if he took his foot off the gas just a little. He's got three kids now. He's got a production company. He's a global brand. There are a million other things that require his attention. But winners don't think about that when it's time to get ready to play.

The thing about Ray and Steph is that they didn't just go out and bang their head on the wall, like some sort of masochist. They worked hard, but also smart—they were extremely deliberate about the skills they wanted to practice. All of the great ones are. They're always identifying weaknesses in their game and putting their attention there. You're happy with your three-point shot? Work on your handle. Happy with your handle? Add muscle so you can bang down low. There's always something you can add. What's the thing you're working on today?

I've seen some guys who are too one-dimensional about what they work on. They're content to be elite at just one facet of the game—and while that's better than nothing, it's not the way to greatness. Besides, while deliberately focusing on your weaknesses may be uncomfortable—it means admitting you *have* weaknesses, which not everyone can do—it's where you see the fastest results. There's no quicker way to see practice pay off than practicing the weakest part of your game. And you aren't just practicing the skill—you're practicing being honest with yourself about what needs work. You're cultivating those habits that you're going to need in crunch time: Passion. Intensity. Focus. When I was coming up, I had a coach who reminded us not to dribble over the out-of-bounds line even during practice, even when we were messing around. You have to know where that line is like it's second nature—and you have to avoid it like it's electrified—or else it's going to come back to bite you in a game, when the stakes are real. Everything about practice is like that. They say "you play the way you practice" for a reason.

Yet guys like Steph and Ray are probably the exceptions. They're anomalies. I've seen so many guys get all the way there. Guys as talented or potentially even more talented than them, who almost accomplish their dreams, who get so close, then stop working—and everything falls apart. That's why you have to build up practicing like any other habit. It's your defense against entropy and irrelevancy. You've made a habit out of brushing your teeth every morning, whatever the weather is outside, however you're feeling that particular day—because oral hygiene is important to overall health. Practice has to be just the same way. It's important to your overall game. You have to head into that gym and put up those shots however you're feeling, whether you're down in the dumps over failure or feeling complacent and satisfied over success. Failing to practice catches up with you sooner than you think. And that goes for any field you're in.

Jascha Heifetz, one of the most famous violinists of the twentieth century, said, "If I don't practice one day, I know it; two days, the critics know it; three days, the public knows it." And that's my experience, too—elite skills fall off so fast if they aren't maintained. One of the saddest things you'll see in the NBA is young players who have struggled all their lives to make the league, finally make it, and then let themselves slide. And when they do, there are plenty of hungrier players ready to take their place. If you want to succeed, at anything, you have to live it.

One of the most surefire ways to keep that fire lit is to make putting in the work part of your daily ritual. You rarely hear about it from NBA players—people think it's more of a baseball or a hockey thing—but we *all* have some sort of ritual or routine. How else could we maintain the kind of discipline it takes to play at that level? That's part of what Ray's set list of shots was all about—building that ritual into his life, every day, so that he wouldn't skip it any more than he'd skip brushing his teeth in the morning.

And if you do it day after day, you see results. That doesn't mean you're guaranteed to start winning championships— remember, there are no guarantees like that. But you are going to start seeing yourself getting stronger, smarter, quicker. And the more you see that, the more you'll be motivated to keep building on it. You'll know that you're building something special. That's what kept me out on the court in the Texas heat growing up. That's what kept me in the gym after practice. I didn't know where this would end up, but I knew I was building something I could be proud of.

When you really put in the work and get to watch it pay off, it feels so good. The first time I really, really felt that was when I was playing in a summer tournament at Roosevelt High School in Dallas, the summer after my freshman year of high school. I was taking basketball really seriously for the first time. I was working on my game every day. I was in the weight room—I had a coach who picked me up and took me to the gym to lift weights for the first time. That was the year Antawn Jamison was blowing up at UNC, and I remember working in the gym to copy his moves. I could see myself getting stronger and more skilled. I was getting addicted to the work. I took all this practice, weight training, and conditioning, and finally got to implement them against the best competition in the state. And, by God, it worked.

In the tournament semifinals, we were down big, I think by 20-something points. And during timeouts, I just remember staring at this trophy—the tournament MVP trophy—that they had sitting on the scorer's table, courtside. I don't know why, but I was fixated on that damn trophy. I wanted it so bad. Maybe it felt like it would be validation for all the work I put in. I don't know, but I know that when we were down big I still couldn't stop obsessing over that trophy. And you know what? I dug deep, drew on all of that strength training and conditioning I put in, and went out and got it. We came back in the game, we won the tournament, and I got the MVP trophy. I put it in my room, and I still kept staring at it. Because now it was proof that when I really put in the work, I'd get the rewards. And then I started to wonder: What else can I get?

If you want success at any level, that's got to be your mindset. If you want the rewards and you're not putting in the work, you're kidding yourself. If you're not going to do the work, then why were you even bothering with this book?

It should excite you when you have the chance to improve yourself. I was always motivated by maximizing my potential. I wanted to be successful in every game, and the only way to do that was to work my butt off. That's why it's important to find what you love and try to do that, because it won't seem like work and you won't mind putting in the time necessary to be great. Because that's a lot of time.

If you want to excel, you're not going to spend most of your time cutting down nets and spraying champagne—you're going to be spending most of your time doing that work. So you'd better figure out a way to enjoy it, even when it hurts. I love the way Jerry Seinfeld put it once: "Your blessing in life is when you find the torture you're comfortable with . . . it's work, it's exercise. Find the torture you're comfortable with and you'll do well."

I love that because it's realistic. No one is telling you that hitting the weight room or running sprints is going to feel good. It's not gonna be fun, probably most of the time. Sometimes it'll feel like torture. But if you really want to excel, you find ways of making it comfortable. Usually after a workout, I'd sit there and visualize myself being successful. Using those moves we had been working on all summer in the game when the season started. Seeing myself knocking down that crucial free throw at the line. Visualizing myself lifting the trophy. Doing the work allows you to go through all of these emotions and actions in your mind before you go through them on the court.

Those are the results. But then there's just the pure feeling of being at the top of your game—whatever level you're on—and knowing it. Being in the zone.

Everyone talks about being in the zone. But you only get there through intense, vigorous work and single-minded focus. It's the consistency of practice that enables you to perform and function throughout a game, or a moment when your mind is completely unclouded. The only thing going through your mind when you release a shot is follow-through and good balance. You can tune out hecklers, twenty thousand screaming fans, the fear of failure— everything. Like everything else in sports, people see the results of being in the zone—"Damn, he's on another level out there!"—but they rarely see the work that goes into achieving that plane of consciousness.

People would always ask me how it feels to just be in it, and it's really indescribable. You're too busy being in the moment to de- scribe it—and the minute you think about what's happening, it's gone. Being in the zone is about being completely present. But you don't get to that state of mind without preparing for it, day in and day out. You can't force it—but you can make room for it. In a way, though, that state of total presence is your reward for put- ting in the work. Most people who suit up for a sport aren't going to win a championship. But whatever level you're playing at, you can experience that state of total absorption and total presence— if you prepare for it.

And it's even more special when a team as a whole hits that level. You have to put in the reps as an individual—and a team has to put in its reps, too. You have to practice communicating, rotating on defense, hitting the open guy on offense. Like I've written to you before, it can take practice after practice—sometimes year after year—for a group to jell.

Think about how the Spurs spent years and years slogging away to eventually be in a position to beat us. In 2012, they lost in the Western Conference Finals. The next year, we beat them for the championship. The year after that, they came all the way back and got their revenge on us. It was a slow build for them—a war of attrition. They were an insanely talented group of guys, with one of the all-time great coaches in Gregg Popovich. But in an era of "superteams" that came together through free agency, the Spurs kept the same group of players, and just grinded methodically, year after year, until they took us down. It hurt—losing always does. But I've always respected hard work, even from my adversaries, and I have a deep respect for what they put in to get to the highest level. Plus having pretty much five Hall of Famers helps, too!

All of these letters have been about putting in the work. Cultivating your mind. Pushing your body. Mastering your ego. Learning to mesh with your teammates. None of it comes easy—if it did, there would be nothing impressive about being a champion. I can tell you all about it, I can try to inspire you, but I can't do it for you. What comes next in your story is up to you.

I've mentioned it before, but if you haven't seen *The Last Dance*, the documentary about Michael Jordan and the Bulls at the end of their second three-peat, you should. Then you should watch it again. Watch it like game film. Start and stop it a million times. There's all sorts of subtle stuff in there that you can miss if you're not watching closely. There's one thing that I caught. Jordan is with his teammates in the huddle at the very beginning of their last playoff run. They all put their hands in. Then Jordan says to them—not yelling, but very quietly, a motto for the game and the season—"Starts with hard work, ends in champagne."

Starts with hard work, ends in champagne.

How much hard work?

As much as it takes.

It's as simple as that. Few if any athletes have ever had as much talent as MJ—but no one ever worked harder. He added fifteen extra pounds of muscle to help his team get past the Detroit Pistons in the '90s. He learned a new offensive system, the triangle, to take away opponents' ability to beat the Bulls by double- and triple-teaming him when Phil Jackson came on board. He learned how to become a passer, a playmaker, the league's top defender. As his business empire grew, he learned how to be a salesman and an executive and a maker of hard decisions. He had to spend hours talking to reporters, responding to criticism, figuring out how to be a communicator and a role model. Everything he did was a chance to identify and overcome another weakness, a chance to become world-class at something new. None of that was easy. None of that could just be "picked up" on the fly.

Some people look at Jordan and see one of the most gifted

athletes of all time. Sure—but I look at him and see a person who never stopped learning. I see all of those hundreds, thousands of hours of work.

I mentioned that when I was with the Heat, Coach Spoelstra gave me Malcolm Gladwell's book *Outliers*, which famously says that it takes roughly ten thousand hours of practice to reach expertise in any given skill. Another great book on the idea of achieving excellence in your field is *Mastery* by Robert Greene, which says it takes closer to twenty thousand hours. But look, those are just rules of thumb. There are plenty of people who put in even more and still never make it to the mountaintop. If you could trade X number of hours for X amount of greatness, 100 percent guaranteed, greatness wouldn't be that impressive.

There's no way of knowing exactly what it's going to cost when you set out on the journey. Maybe that's just why the journey is so hard—and so rewarding when you reach your destination. Maybe all you can say is: *It takes what it takes.*

# CONCLUSION

lay every game like it's your last.

You've probably heard that a million times. It's a cliché, so you dismiss it. It's a way to motivate you, so you use it.

But you never really let it hit you. Because the idea is just too sensitive, the truth too painful to actually consider. I know from experience, because the thing I'd been building to for my whole life—being in the NBA—was taken away from me in an instant. Suddenly. Cruelly. A freak medical issue. Nothing I did wrong. But there I was, off the court and on the IR list. There's a quote that goes around the internet these days. Sometimes they attribute it to the movie *The Sandlot*, though I don't remember it being there. It does *feel* like it belongs there, though:

At some point in your childhood, you and your friends went outside to play together for the last time and nobody knew it.

My last game in the NBA was against the Spurs on a Wednesday night in February. We didn't win. We didn't play particularly well. It was a pretty ordinary day in an ordinary season in the history of the league. All I was thinking about was getting the team good enough to make a run for a championship after the All-Star Game. LeBron had left and was defending the Eastern Conference title with the Cavs.

I think we had the stuff. I think we could have done it. What a series that would have been. One for the ages.

It was not to be.

In the winter of 2015, doctors found a blood clot in one of my lungs. I thought it was just one of those small health setbacks any athlete has from time to time. I took some time to recover and finished out the season.

A year later, they found another blood clot in my leg. I thought I'd rehab, beat it, come back stronger for the playoff run. It didn't happen. The problem never cleared up. A blood clot can break away and travel through your circulatory system—something that's more likely to happen when you're exercising at high intensity, like on a basketball court. If it lodges in an artery that carries blood to the lungs, it can cause a pulmonary embolism. If it lodges in the heart, it can cause a heart attack. If it lodges in the brain, it can cause a stroke. The doctors told me, "If you go back on the court, you're risking your life." And I'll be honest with you, it took me a while to understand what the doctors were telling me. We weren't talking about a "career-ending injury." Playing basketball could literally kill me. My first thought was, "The game *is* my life." There were actual moments when risking my life seemed like it made more sense than giving up basketball.

It's moments like that that teach you the importance of having a large purpose and passion for what you do. It forced me to reexamine why I played, what the game meant to me, and, most of all, who I was as a person. That spring, I was ruled out for the playoffs. I still thought the problem might clear up over the summer, and I'd be back for next year, but no. I'd played my last game, and I didn't even know it.

What happened? Could it have been avoided? Since I was in high school, I worked my ass off, I gave my all to the game, I tried to control everything that I possibly could—my conditioning, my diet, my relationships with my teammates. But the thing that ended my career was completely beyond my control—a blood clot just a few centimeters wide. After all I'd given the game, why did it have to happen to me?

"Theirs not to reason why," the poem goes.

*It is what it is.*

We don't control what happens to us, the Stoics say. We only control how we respond.

I thought the hardest thing I had ever done was win an NBA

championship. It turns out that winning a championship was much, much easier than coming to terms with the fact that I'd never play basketball again. It was like a part of me died. It was like a piece of life was cut out of me, stolen, taken before its time.

Some people look at me and the success I've had and say, "Hey, man, great career. You should be proud. Your health is more important."

It's true. On one level, I know they're right. I'm grateful for what I've achieved, and there are much worse ways to go out. Imagine snapping your leg on the court and being carried off on a stretcher in unbelievable pain. Imagine finding out one morning in training camp that you've been cut, nice knowing you, clean out your locker. Rationally, I know that I'm among the luckiest people to ever play this game.

But as you know, there is something about this game that is beyond rational. That is beyond reasonable. Sport is an obsession. It's a deep love. It's a profound expression. They say *ball is life*. It is. So when it goes away, no matter how it goes away, there is real grief.

For me, basketball was the daily fulfillment of doing what I was born to do. Health? The injuries I've played through, the risks I've taken on the court, the battles I've fought . . . the way I thought about it, I risked my health a little every time I laced up my shoes. And even though this was far more serious—even though I knew the difference between something that could put me on crutches and something that could kill me—it was a hard pill to swallow.

But ball is life. Endings are a part of life. And all endings hurt. I don't know how the hurt I felt, knowing that my career was over, compares to the hurt other athletes have felt in the same place. You only get to feel it once, and only for yourself. But whether we go out kicking and screaming, or whether we go out gracefully, we all leave eventually.

Whether it's your last year of varsity lacrosse, the end of your college swimming career, or the day you have to face the fact that you're never going to be called up to the majors, eventually, inevitably, our status as athletes changes. Some of us will blow out knees and never be able to take another jump shot, some of us get in car accidents and will never run a marathon, some of us get older and take up golf instead of full-contact tackle football.

Stepping away from the game challenged me at the soul level. But it also opened up my soul in new ways. It's made me realize sports isn't just winning, it's not just getting paid, it's not just the hunger to improve, as important as all of those things are. It's also about friendships, the daily practice of doing what you love, pulling through as a team, pushing yourself past your limits. Learning how to work together for one directed goal and feeling the triumphs and defeats that go with it.

It has been a challenging journey, but I wouldn't want a life without challenges. I felt the same way when I played the game. Those championships were so sweet because they cost us so much. And building my life after basketball is so sweet because it's the hardest thing I've done. I've had my depressed days, my pity parties, all of that. But what you learn playing the game stays with you, and one thing I learned was how to get up when I've been knocked down, no matter how much it hurts. You can't play successfully at the highest level unless you hate losing. You can't make it to the highest level unless you absorb a lot of losses on the way. Leaving the game is always painful—but playing the game is also a powerful preparation for the eventual pain of leaving it.

As I've told you again and again throughout these letters, if the only thing you're taking from your sport is stronger muscles or better conditioning, you're missing out on so much of what it has to offer you. It's offering you the chance to learn how to communicate honestly, to absorb criticism and grow, to lose gracefully, to win humbly, to push yourself past the physical and mental limits you thought you had. My life is so much richer because of all that basketball taught me. And those riches are a part of me now. I get to keep them whether or not I'm on the court.

Now I have a team at home—five children. I try my best to lead them by example every day. And I look forward to thinking about what's next for myself—because the way I see it, basketball was just the first quarter of my life. Now I'm on a mission to find the new things that will bring out my best and keep teaching me in the way the game did.

I always imagined that my career would end like David Robinson's had, winning a championship in my last year of playing ball. Even if I was forced out by injuries, I had hoped for something like Peyton Manning's last Super Bowl, a gutsy, broken, limping-to-the-finish-line win, against all odds, and then a retirement not a moment too soon. Even if I didn't get to go out with a championship, I would have loved to go out on my own terms, to have a victory lap like D-Wade or Dirk.

But again, that was not to be.

Not mine to reason why.

It is what it is.

I was disappointed. Angry. Sad.

But all I could do was react, move forward, tackle what's next. Because . . . life.

The end of one journey sets up the beginning of another. LeBron is right when he says that we are "More Than an Athlete." You know what David Robinson is doing now? He runs a groundbreaking school called the Carver Academy, which has helped thousands of kids in San Antonio. Bill Bradley? He went on to become a U.S. senator. Gerald Ford had a chance to play in the NFL, but he chose law and then politics instead, eventually finding himself in the Oval Office. Steve Young runs an investment firm. Maya Moore has managed to become an incredible advocate for social justice and criminal justice reform. Stephen Jackson thought that hosting a podcast would be an interesting career after more than a decade in the NBA. He had no sense of what destiny would be soon calling for him to do—but when his boyhood friend George Floyd was brutally murdered by the police in 2020, he immediately understood.

We are more than athletes, but that's not a knock on athletes. It's a compliment: What better preparation could there be for the business world, for politics, for leadership, for fighting for justice than the gauntlet we have been through as players over these long years? Every practice, every snap, every victory, every loss is setting you up for something, whether you understand it or not. Don't let anyone tell you to "shut up and dribble." You not only have every right to participate and contribute to the direction of your country and the future, I would argue that it's your *obligation* to do so.

It took me a while, a lot of thinking, a lot of talking, and even writing this book to come around to the idea that actually, maybe, the way I went out was perfect.

That ordinary midseason game against the Spurs wasn't glamorous. *But it was basketball.* A normal routine night playing basketball against an old adversary. It didn't have any expectations, any specialness beyond the privilege of getting to play the game in front of tens of thousands of fans. It just was. I gave it my all. It was a game just like hundreds of games I'd played over the years, just like games you've played, too. I didn't give it my all because I knew it was my last game. I gave it my all because I chose to play every game like it was my last. And then, without my realizing it, it was. I was hungry. I felt the familiar burn in my muscles in the fourth quarter. I put my ego at the service of my team. I picked my teammates up when they made mistakes, and they did the same for me. I was present. I was locked in. I felt every tick of the shot clock.

You can choose to play like that, every single time you lace 'em up. Play like it's your last. Put in the work even when you don't want to, even when your body and mind are screaming at you. When someone offers you the easy way out, take the hard way. Be present to the game and to your teammates. Remember that the game—whichever game you pursue—is bigger than you, and never forget that you are built for bigger things, too.

And if you do that, you may still be disappointed about how it all ends, like I was. But you won't have a single regret.

# ACKNOWLEDGMENTS

This book was a tremendous challenge that took a total team effort, and I am forever grateful to those who helped me on this wonderful journey toward making it a reality.

I'd like to thank my wife and kids for aiding me and encouraging me when times got tough and it seemed out of reach.

I'd like to thank agents Anthony Mattero and Justin Castillo at CAA, for bringing up the opportunity and making it happen. I can't lie. When the idea first came up of writing a book, it seemed like something too far off, too big a reach. Through many meetings and phone calls we eventually found the idea. Thank you guys for your efforts. I'd also like to thank the late and great Henry Thomas, my former agent, one of the greatest men I've known, truly one of the good guys. May you rest in peace.

Thanks to Ryan Holiday, for those countless hours of conversations, voice memos, and work on this book. The first lunch sit-down we had, I knew you were the guy to collaborate with, and going through this process with you has been a great learning experience. Figuring out how to get this message across is something that I will always take with me. You have helped make this process fun and enjoyable through the challenges.

To Scott Moyers and his team at Penguin, for those many conversations from the inception of the book to sharpening it and going through every word in every chapter. The countless emails back and forth let me know that you all care just as much as I do about getting this message out. Writing and editing can be a tedious process, but you all have helped make it an enjoyable experience. Working with you guys has been wonderful, and I am looking forward to the future with you all. We've got a lot more work to do!!!!!

I'd also like to acknowledge the fact that you can do surprising things if you put in the effort. This book is living proof.

# INDEX

Abdul-Jabbar, Kareem, 37
adversity, xix–xxii, 26–27, 182. *See also*
    losing
Alabama Crimson Tide, 95
Aldridge, LaMarcus, 25
Ali, Muhammad, 25
Allen, Ray, 104, 126, 204
    2013 NBA Finals, xiii–xiv, 20–22,
        159–60, 166, 199–201
Allen, Robert, 13–14
analytic revolution, 64–66
ancient Olympic Games, 77, 95
Antetokounmpo, Giannis, 64–65
Anthony, Carmelo
    2008 Olympic Games, 89, 164–65
    life after basketball, 71
anxiety, 136n
*Any Given Sunday* (movie), 34
Apple, 31–32
Aristotle, 153
Arizona State Sun Devils, 41
arrogance, 51, 143, 189
asking questions, 8

Atlanta Braves, 58–59
Atlanta Falcons, 35–36
attendance figures NBA games, average, 5

Bad News Bears, 38
ballet, 70
*ball is life*, 214–15
Barea, J. J., 93
Barkley, Charles "Chuck," 82–83, 144
Barry, Rick, 49
basketball goals, 6–7
basketball language, 72, 74–76
basketball scholarship, 36–37
Battier, Shane
    on championship rings, 104
    mental preparation of, 66–68
    teamwork, 83, 162, 168–69
batting average 400, 183
Beijing Summer Olympics (2008), 12, 88,
        100–102, 164–65
"being in the zone," 207–8
Belichick, Bill, 52
Belluz, Julia, 131–32

Bennett, Tony, 182
Biggie Smalls, 38
Bird, Sue, 106–7
Birdsong, Otis, 37
Bishop, Leonard, 110–12, 120, 122–23
bitterness, 143, 145–46
Black Lives Matter, 218
*Bleacher Report*, 145
body, care of, 124–39
Bosh, Adrienne, xxi
Bosh, Noel, 36–37, 184
Boston Celtics, 69
Bradley, Bill, 217
Brady, Tom, 50, 70, 95
    self-care of, 126, 131–32
breathing exercises, 133
Bryant, Kobe, 17, 95, 191
    2008 Olympic Games, 89, 164–65
    criticism of, 150
    visualization and practice, 197–98, 199
*Business Insider*, 129–30
bust your ass, 17–18

Calderón, José, 167
*Captain Class, The* (Walker), 113–14
care of self, 124–39
Carter, Maverick, 128
Carver Academy, 217
celebrations, 177
Central Arkansas Bears, 23
Chalmers, Mario, 83–84
champions vs. runner-ups, 25
Chandler, Tyson, 40
cheating the game, 16–17
Cheesecake Factory, 126
chess player language, 72–73
Chicago Bulls, 49, 115–16, 189
    *The Last Dance*, 193, 208–10
*Chop Wood Carry Water* (Medcalf), 70
Churchill, Winston, 69–70, 76–77
"clarity of why," 31–32
Clemens, Roger, 58
Cleveland Cavaliers, xx, 129, 212

coding (computer programming), 68
communication, 72–90
    after losses, 81–847
    leadership and, 76–79, 86–89, 110
    practicing, 80–81
    sports/war analogy, 77–79
concussions in NFL, 136
conditioning, 13–14, 18, 22–23, 24, 27,
    137–38, 205
coworkers vs. friends, 117–18
creativity, 62–63
criticism (critics), 140–57
    communication and, 86–87
    leaders and, 153–54
    listening to, 151–52
    media and, 144–47, 150–51
Crohn's disease, 4
*cultivate*, 61–62
cultivating the mind, 55–71, 85
    data analytics, 64–66
    reading, 55–57, 61
    student-athletes, 59–60, 63–64
Curry, Michael, 167–68
Curry, Seth, 49
Curry, Stephen, 46, 49, 195
    hard work and practice of, 190,
        201–2

Dallas Cowboys, 189
Dallas Mavericks, 2011 NBA Finals,
    xv–xix, 40, 146, 180–81
dance, 70
"Dancing in the Dark" (song), 45
D'Antoni, Mike, 4, 14–15
data analytics, 64–66
David, Walter, 37
Davis, Anthony, 74
de la Pava, Sergio, 192
Denver Nuggets, 106–7
depression, 136n
Detroit Pistons, 49, 209
diet, 26, 131–32
discipline, 42, 204

Dončić, Luka, 73
"don't get too high, don't get too
   low," 176
"do the work," 194–210
   "being in the zone," 207–8
   Bulls and *The Last Dance*, 208–10
   importance of practice, 197–207
Dragić, Goran, xx
Dream Team (1992 United States men's
   Olympic basketball team), 164
Drew League, 37
drive, 46, 47. *See also* hunger
Duke Blue Devils, 41
"dumb jock," 57–58
Duncan, Tim, 17, 165
   2013 NBA Finals, xii–xiv, 22, 163–64
Durant, Kevin "KD," 66, 195
   2012 NBA Finals, xii
   criticism of, 143

Eastern Conference Finals
   1991, 193
   2010, 115–16
   2013, 155
   2019, 178–79
ego vs. self-confidence, 106–7
ego, keeping in check, 54, 91–108
   communication and, 86
   Raptors 2003 rookie year, 96–98
   USA World Championship Team
      (2006), 98–102
Eisenhower, Dwight, 86
Embiid, Joel, 178–79
Emery, Ray, 70
Empty light, 19–20
endurance, 18–20, 24
energy reserves, 12, 13–15, 19–20
*en passant*, 72–73
Epictetus, 194
ESPN, 93–94, 201
excuse-making, 18, 79, 88, 174,
      184–85
exhaustion, 11–28, 45, 196

Facebook, 183
failure, 26, 38–39, 94, 95–96, 142.
   *See also* adversity; losing
fame, 31–32, 37–39
"familiar territory," 21
fan noise, 4–5
fatigue, 11–28, 45, 196
finding your why, 29–43
   2019 New Orleans Saints game,
      34–36
   fame and popularity, 37–39
   love of the game, 33–34, 43
Floyd, George, 218
focus, 26, 50, 62–63
football language, 72
Ford, Gerald, 217
Formula 1, 49–50
free throws, 30, 55, 56, 148, 154,
      195, 206
friends vs. coworkers, 117–18
fruits and vegetables, 131–32
Fujita, Scott, 35–36

Gaines, Cork, 129–30
game tape, 56, 62, 117, 177
"garbage time," 47
Garnett, Kevin, 69, 169, 198–99
genetics, 127, 129
Georgia Tech Yellow Jackets, 23, 96–97,
      176–77
gift of hunger, 44–54
Gilmore, Artis, 37
Ginobili, Manu, xii–xiv
Gladwell, Malcolm, 56, 210
Gleason, Steve, 36
goals, 6–7. *See also* finding your why
Goggins, David, 18–19
Golden State Warriors, 129, 137, 142,
      165, 201
*Great Gatsby, The* (Fitzgerald), 63
Green, Danny, xiv, 74, 93
Green, Draymond, 49, 137
Green Bay Packers, 57

Greene, Robert, 210
Griffin, Shaquem, 195
grind, 13
grit, 22–23
guitar lessons, 68

Hamilton, Lewis, 49–50
Hamilton, Rip, 17
Hardaway, Tim, Jr., 49
Harden, James, xii–xiv, 50, 65
hard work, 194–210
    "being in the zone," 207–8
    Bulls and *The Last Dance*,
        208–10
    importance of practice,
        197–207
Harry Potter, 63
haters, 2, 39–40, 140, 142, 148, 151.
    *See also* criticism
heart attacks, 212–13
Heat. *See* Miami Heat
Heifetz, Jascha, 203–4
Hernandez, Jose, 58–59
Hewitt, Paul, 96
Hill, Thomas, 6–7, 29–30, 42
hip-hop, 37–38
Hitler, Adolf, 76–77
Hitzlsperger, Thomas, 195
Holyfield, Evander, 70
honesty, 152
Houston Rockets, 65
Howard, Dwight, 74, 101
Howard, Juwan, 88, 113
human brain, 62, 64
humility, 102, 104, 140, 152, 160
hunger, 44–54, 65
Hunger Games, 46
Hurley, Bobby, 41
Hurricane Katrina, 35–36
Hutchins Elementary School, 33

"If" (Kipling), 174–75
Iguodala, Andre, 105

*Iliad* (Homer), 77–78
*Illmatic* (Nas album), 38
Indiana Pacers, 20, 155
injuries, 3–4, 41–42, 134–35, 138
    2016 blood clot, xx–xxi, 3–4,
        212–13
*Inner Game of Tennis, The* (Gallwey), 70
inner voice, 2, 4, 5, 25
Instagram, 183
Irving, Kyrie, 83, 165
*It is what it is*, 213

Jackson, Bo, 3–4
Jackson, Phil, 153, 161, 209
Jackson, Stephen, 217
James, LeBron, 120, 217
    2008 Olympic Games, 89,
        164–65
    2010–11 season, 115–16, 160–61
    2011 NBA Finals, xvi–xix
    2013 NBA Finals, xii–xiv
    2014 move to Cleveland, xx, 212
    Big Three, xvi–xix, xx, 144,
        160–61
    criticism of, 143, 144
    gift of hunger, 51, 54
    photographic memory of, 57–58
    self-care and recovery of, 124–25, 126,
        128, 129–30, 132, 133
    teamwork, 74, 162
Jamison, Antawn, 205
Jemison, Mae, 70
Jeter, Derek, 95
Johnson, Dennis, 37
Johnson, Larry, 25
Johnson, Marques, 37
Johnson, Randy, 58
Jordan, Michael "MJ," 144
    criticism of, 150
    gift of hunger, 49, 51
    *The Last Dance*, 193, 208–10
    *Space Jam*, 163
jump shot, 6, 148

Karney, Mike, 35–36, 43
Kerr, Steve, 105
Kidd, Jason, xv–xvi, 180
Kipling, Rudyard, 161–62, 174–75
Krzyzewski, Mike "Coach K," 4, 88–89,
    100–101, 162

Laimbeer, Bill, 193
Lanier High School, 184
Larry O'Brien Championship Trophy,
    158–59
Last Dance, The (documentary), 193,
    208–10
leaders (leadership), 109–23
    criticism and, 153–54
    fallibility of, 121–22
    importance of communication, 76–79,
        86–89, 110
    leading by example, 110–12,
        115–17, 120
    learning to follow, 112–13
    preparing to change, 119–21
    traits of, 113–14
learning, 7–8
learning the language, 72–75
Leonard, Kawhi, 134–35
    2019 Eastern Conference Finals,
        178–79
Leslie, Lisa, 195
Letters to a Young Jazz Musician
    (Marsalis), 7–8
Letters to a Young Poet (Rilke),
    7–8
Lewis, Michael, 53
Lewis, Rashard, 104
Lillard, Damian, 70
Lincoln High School, 6–7, 13–14,
    48, 52, 96, 110–12, 126,
    184, 191
listening
    to criticism, 151–52
    importance of, 89–90
    to your body, 135–36

Little League World Series, 178
live everything, 8–9
"load management," 135–36
Lombardi Trophy, 34
Los Angeles Dodgers, 58–59
Los Angeles Lakers, 161, 188–89, 191
Los Angeles Rarms, 34–35
Los Angeles Sparks, 12–13
losing (losses), 174–93
    communication after, 81–84, 87
    making excuses, 18, 79, 88, 174,
        184–85
    motivation after, 180, 181
    sore losers, 183–85, 191
losing streaks, 176
Love, Kevin, 60–61, 136n
love of the game, 2–3, 9, 33–34, 43
Lucas, Maurice, 37
luck, 5–6, 30, 56, 181, 198–99
Lynch, Marshawn, 11–12

McDonald's Quarter Pounders, 126
McGinnis, George, 37
McLendon, Steve, 70
Maddux, Greg, 58–59
Malone, Karl, 193
Mancias, Mike, 130
Manning, Peyton, 183, 217
Martin, Darrick, 112–13, 167
Massachusetts Institute of Technology
    (MIT), 70
Mastery (Greene), 210
Mays, Robert, 35
media, 144–45, 150–51
memory, 57–58
mens sana in corpore sano, 64, 138
mental fatigue, 12–13, 16
mental health, 136n
mental preparation, 55–71
    data analytics, 64–66
    reading, 55–57, 61
    student-athletes, 59–60, 63–64
mental toughness, 67–71

Miami Heat. *See also specific players*
    2010–11 debut season, 39–40, 55–56,
        102–3, 114–16, 144, 160–61
    NBA Finals, xv–xix, 40, 146,
        180–81
    2012 NBA Finals, xii, 186–87
    2013–14 season
        Eastern Conference Finals, 155
        NBA Finals, xii–xiv, 20–22, 102,
            159–60, 162–64, 165–66,
            187–88, 199–201
    2015–16 season, 121–22
    blood clot, xx–xxi, 3–4, 212–13
    2019 season
        retirement, 214–17
        retirement of jersey, xix, xxi–xxii,
            158–59, 161, 172
    adversity, xix–xxii
    Big Three, xvi–xix, xx, 114–15, 144,
        160–61
    criticism and, 144, 145–46, 147
    importance of communication, 74–75,
        80, 83–84
    leadership of, 120, 121–22
    team rituals, 117–18
    teamwork, 167–70
Michigan Wolverines, 88
Mighty Ducks, 38
mindfulness routine, 133
misery, xvi–xvii
mission statement, 32
Mitchell, Sam, 98, 163, 199
Moawad, Trevor, 194
*Monday Night Football*, 35
money, 31–32, 35, 39, 103, 127, 141
Moore, Maya, 217
Musk, Elon, 50
MVPs (Most Valuable Players), xiv, 52,
    201, 205
Myers, Bob, 137

name on the front of the jersey,
    158–73
Napoleon Bonaparte, 78

Nas, 38
Nash, Steve, 198
National Basketball Association
    Awards—Larry O'Brien
        Championship Trophy, 158–59
National Invitation Tournament (2003),
    176–77
Nazis, 69–70, 76–77
NBA bro-code, 16, 21
NBA draft, 189
NBA Finals
    2011, xv–xix, 40, 180–81
    2012, xii, 186–87
    2013, xii–xiv, 20–22, 102, 159–60,
        162–64, 165–66, 187–88,
        199–201
    winner-take-all scenarios, xv
NBA G League, 93
*NBA on TNT*, 82–83
NBA Western Conference All-Stars
    (1979), 37
NCAA scholarships, 59–60
NCAA tournament, 47, 176, 178, 182
New Orleans Saints, 34–36
New Orleans Superdome, 35–36
"new thing," 53, 216
New York Yankees, 189
NFC Championship Game (2019),
    34–35
NFL player concussions, 136
noise of fans, 4–5
North Carolina Tar Heels, 205
Nowitzki, Dirk, xv–xvi, 180, 198

Oakley, Charles, 144
off-season training, 25
Oklahoma City Thunder, 2012 NBA
    Finals, xii, 186–87
Olympic Games
    ancient, 77, 95
    1992, 164
    2008, 12, 88, 100–102, 164–65
O'Neal, Shaquille, 150, 165, 191
*Outliers* (Gladwell), 56, 210

out-of-the-box learning, 70–71
Overbeck, Carla, 114
overconfidence, 176

pain, 13, 17, 22, 25–26
Parcells, Bill, 192
Parker, Candace, 12–13, 17, 70
Parker, Tony, xii–xiv, 83
patience, 62–63
Patton, George S., 79
Paul, Chris, 73
Payton, Sean, 34–36
personal goals, 6–7. *See also* finding
    your why
Philadelphia Phillies, 41
Philadelphia 76ers, 105, 178–79
Phoenix Suns, xx, 14–15
Pippen, Scottie, 23, 144
pitchers, 58–59
Pittsburgh Steelers, 41
"play every game like it's your last,"
    211–12
Popovich, Gregg, xii–xiv, 165, 208
popularity, 37–39
possessions and communication, 75–76
practice, 21–22, 29–30, 44, 197–207
problem-solving, 153
pulmonary embolism, 212
purpose, 40–41, 44–45, 50–51, 213.
    *See also* finding your why
pushing your limits, 18–20

quitting, 92

racism, 148
Randolph, Zach, 169
Rapinoe, Megan, 95, 107
Raptors. *See* Toronto Raptors
reading, 55–57, 61, 146
rebounds (rebounding), 15–17, 45
records, 192–93
Redeem Team (2008 United States men's
    Olympic basketball team), 88,
    100–102, 164–65

Redick, J. J., 23
resentment, 145–46
respect, 189–90
retired number, xix, xxi–xxii, 158–59,
    161, 172
Riley, Pat, xi–xxii, 4, 161
    1987 NBA Finals, 188–89
    2011 NBA Finals, xv–xix
    2013 NBA Finals, xii–xiv, 22, 159–60
    *The Winner Within*, 107
Rilke, Rainer Maria, 7–8
Rivers, Austin, 49
Roberson, Ken, 25
Robinson, David, 216–17
Robinson, Jackie, 195
Rodgers, Aaron, 57–58
Rodman, Dennis, 23
"role players," 160
Roman Colosseum, 46, 74
Rondo, Rajon, 74–75
Roosevelt, Teddy, 156–57
Roosevelt High School, 204–5
Rucker Park (New York City), 37
runner-ups vs. champions, 25
Ruth, Babe, 128

Saban, Nick, 95
sacrifice, xvii, xviii
San Antonio Spurs, 66–67, 208, 212
    2013 NBA Finals, xii–xiv, 20–22, 102,
        162–64, 165–66, 187–88
    Leonard at, 134–35
*Sandlot, The* (movie), 211–12
scholarships, 59–60
Schumacher, Michael, 50
second-guessing, 142
self-care, 124–39
self-centeredness, 98–100. *See also* ego,
    keeping in check
self-confidence, 143–44
    ego vs., 106–7
self-criticism, 68–69
self-doubts, 68–69
self-esteem, 39, 191

self-interest, 171–72
selfishness, 100–102, 171
self-motivation, after losing, 180, 181
self-talk, 2, 4, 5, 25
Seneca the Younger, 190–91
Shakur, Tupac, 38
Shazier, Ryan, 41
Sherman, Richard, 59–60
shortcuts, 18
Sikma, Jack, 37
Simmons, Bill, 128
Sinek, Simon, 31–32
sleep, 133–34, 135
smack talking, 44, 69, 147 149
smoking, 135
soccer language, 72
social justice, 71, 218
social media, 144–45, 146, 147, 149
"social survival," 169
sore losers, 183–85, 191
Southeastern Oklahoma State Savage, 23
South Oak Cliff High School, 52
Southwest Airlines, 32
*Space Jam* (movie), 163
Spoelstra, Erik "Spo," 4, 55–56, 84, 103,
    116–17, 121–22, 210
sports analytics, 64–66
sportscasters, 46
*Sports Illustrated*, 58
sportsmanship, 190–91, 226
sports/war analogy, 77–79
Spotify, 37–38
Springsteen, Bruce, 15, 44–45
sprints, 13–15, 24–25
Stanford Cardinal, 59–60, 196
*Start with Why* (Sinek), 31–32
"strength of the team is each individual
    member," 161–62
stretching, 125, 131
stroke, 212–13
student-athletes, 59–60, 63–64
suicide drills, 13–15, 26, 31
Summer Olympics. *See* Olympic Games

Super Bowl XXXVI, 52
Super Bowl XLIV, 36
Super Bowl L, 217
Superdome (New Orleans), 35–36
*supreme conditioning*, 27
sweep away your ego. *See* ego, keeping in
    check

talent, 8, 22–23, 30, 32, 33–34, 47,
    196, 203
tax bill, 140–41
team atmosphere, 84, 85–86
team rituals, 117–18
teamwork, 158–73
    2008 Olympics Games, 164–65
    2013 NBA Finals, 159–60, 162–64,
        165–66
    2019 retirement of jersey, 158–59,
        161, 172
    Miami teammates, 167–70
Tennessee Volunteers, 12
Terry, Jason, 180
Texas Tech Red Raiders, 176
"Think different," 31–32
Thomas, Isiah, 193
Thomas, Kurt, 25
Thompson, David, 37
Thompson, Klay, 49
tiredness, 11–28, 45, 196
*To a Young Jazz Musician: Letters from the
    Road* (Marsalis), 7–8
Toronto Raptors, xviii, 69, 144
    2003 rookie season, 96–98
    2019 Eastern Conference Finals,
        178–79
    leadership, 119
    Martin and leadership, 112–13, 167
    rebounding, 15–16, 18
Tour de France, 129
training, 13–14, 24–25
trash talking, 44, 69, 147 149
trust, 67, 85–86
Twitter, 146, 147, 154

UFC (Ultimate Fighting
    Championship), 156
ultramarathons, 18–19
underdogs, 38, 141, 188
United States men's Olympic basketball
    team
    1992, 164
    2008, 88, 100–102, 164
Urschel, John, 70
USA World Championship Team (2006),
    98–102
Utah Jazz, 121–22

Van Gundy, Jeff, 162
Virginia Cavaliers, 182
Virginia Union Panthers, 23
visualization, 63, 64, 67, 69–70,
    197–98, 206
Vox, 131–32

Wade, Dwyane "D-Wade," 120,
    169–70
    2008 Olympic Games, 89, 164–65
    2010–11 season, 160–61
    2011 NBA Finals, xvi–xix
    Big Three, xvi–xix, xx, 144, 160–61,
        169–70
    criticism of, 144
    self-care and recovery of, 126, 132
    teamwork, 83
Wagner, Dajuan, 3–4
Waitkus, Eddie, 41
Walker, Herschel, 70
Walker, Sam, 113–14

Wallace, Ben, 23
"wanting it more," 46–47
war/sports analogy, 77–79
weaknesses, 58, 202–3
Webb, Spud, 195
weight training, 56, 131, 196, 205
West, Kanye, 98
Westbrook, Russell, xii–xiv, 21
Westphal, Paul, 37
White, Dana, 156
Whiteside, Hassan, 93
whole package, 56
"why?". See finding your why
Williams, Jay, 4
Williams, Serena, 39
Williams, Ted, 183
Williamson, Zion, 41–42
Wilson, Russell, 194
wind sprints, 13–15, 24–25
Winner Within, The (Riley), 107
winning, xvi–xvii, 174–93, 213–14
"win one for the Gipper," 116
"win some, lose some," 46
WNBA, 12–13, 106
Women's World Cup (1999), 114
Wooden, John, 7, 188
Woods, Tiger, 196
working hard. See hard work
World War II, 69–70, 76–77

Young, Steve, 217

Zeno of Elea, 151
Zuckerberg, Mark, 183